I0137005

More Caught
Than Taught

More Caught
Than Taught

Sermons for Lent and Easter
based on the Gospel Lessons
for Cycle A

Paul Hegele

CSS Publishing Company
Lima, Ohio

MORE CAUGHT THAN TAUGHT

FIRST EDITION
Copyright © 2025 by
CSS Publishing Company, Inc.

Published by CSS Publishing Company, Inc., Lima, Ohio 45807. All rights re-served. No part of this publication may be reproduced in any manner what-soever without the prior permission of the publisher, except in the case of brief quotations embodied in critical articles and reviews. Inquiries should be addressed to: CSS Publishing Company, Inc., Permissions Department, 5450 N. Dixie Highway, Lima, Ohio 45807.

Scripture quotations marked (NRSV) are from the New Revised Standard Version of the Bible. Copyright 1989 by the Division of Christian Education of the National Council of the Churches of Christ in the USA, Nashville, Thomas Nelson Publishers © 1989. Used by permission. All rights reserved.

Library of Congress Cataloging-in-Publication Data
Names: Hegele, Paul author
Title: More caught than taught : sermons for Lent and Easter based on the
    gospel lessons for Cycle A / Paul Hegele.
Description: First edition. | Lima, Ohio : CSS Publishing Company, [2025]
Identifiers: LCCN 2025030026 (print) | LCCN 2025030027 (ebook) | ISBN
    9780788031311 paperback | ISBN 9780788031328 adobe pdf
Subjects: LCSH: Bible. Gospels--Sermons | Lenten sermons | Eas-
ter--Sermons
    | Common lectionary (1992). Year A
Classification: LCC BS2555.54 .H44 2025 (print) | LCC BS2555.54 (ebook)
LC record available at https://lccn.loc.gov/2025030026
LC ebook record available at https://lccn.loc.gov/2025030027

For more information about CSS Publishing Company resources, vis-it our website at www.csspub.com, email us at csr@csspub.com, or call (800) 241-4056.

e-book:
ISBN-13: 978-0-7880-3132-8
ISBN-10: 0-7880-3132-5

ISBN-13: 978-0-7880-3131-1
ISBN-10: 0-7880-3131-7   PRINTED IN USA

Dedicated to those intoxicating vessels of joy —
Wes
Aria
Elliott

Contents

More Caught Than Taught

Preaching should never be preachy. A sermon of stories, like its biblical counterpart, the parable, should be savored like good wine. It should stimulate, nourish, be enjoyed, and leave a sweet aftertaste. Jesus told parables that create an earthy environment of stories humble and humorous, knowing that in their relaxed exploring of warmth and wisdom people could make the leap of faith. For faith is more caught than taught.

The Cross You Carry

A pastor I know told about a baptism he once performed. At a baptism's conclusion he always dipped his finger in oil and made the sign of the cross on the baby's head. This baptism was performed outdoors in a park as part of a worship before the congregation's annual church picnic. Following the service, the baby's family celebrated for hours. Family and friends ate burgers and chips and played volleyball under a summer sun. The baby, being only six months old, was left to nap in his stroller and for a time was in the sun. When Mom got him up, whoops. Basted on his forehead was the image of the cross. Mom had forgotten to wash the child's face following his baptism, and the olive oil that the pastor had traced onto his forehead promoted a sunburn. The cross of Christ was imprinted on the child's forehead. For several weeks, until it completely disappeared, that cross was a wonderful reminder of the meaning of baptism, a reminder that the cross of Jesus was 'written' upon us. The baby's mom and dad had to explain the cross to the pediatrician, to the neighbors, and to the stranger in the grocery store. For a few weeks, he was nothing less than a living children's sermon. Sure, it was only a bit of a sunburn, but it was the best basting a child can have — to be marked with the cross of Christ!

If I read the little book of Joel right, God's desire is not that we wear a cross on our forehead, but that it be basted on our hearts. "Rend your heart and not your garments," said Joel (2:13). That's much harder to do, isn't it? It's much easier to rend your clothes than to rend your heart. It's much easier to wear a cross around your neck than it is to bear it daily in everything you do.

Years ago, we witnessed a bloody conflict in the Balkans between Christians and Muslims. Don't assume that Christians were always the good guys. One of the most notorious killers of Muslims was a man by the name of Arkan. When being interviewed by British journalist Martin Bell, Arkan pulled open his shirt to expose a large cross tattoo on his chest. "See," he said, "I am a Christian."

A large cross on your chest does not make you a follower of Jesus. It's much easier to wear your piety outwardly than it is to love God and love your neighbor in the privacy of your own heart. In fact, some people substitute the outward show for the inner devotion. No wonder Jesus counseled, "And when you pray, do not be like the hypocrites, for they love to pray standing in the synagogues and on the street corners to be seen by men. I tell you the truth, they have received their reward in full . . ."

And so, we approach this night with caution. This is not a night for a sham kind of religion. It is a night for focusing on the meaning of our lives in the light of the cross of Jesus Christ--a night for basting the cross on our hearts, even as we place it on our foreheads. Someone gave his life in our behalf.

In the movie *The Last Emperor* a young child was anointed as the last emperor of China. This young emperor lived a life of luxury with a hundred servants at his command. "What happens when you do wrong?" his brother asked.

The boy emperor proudly replied. "When I do wrong, someone else is punished."

To demonstrate this unique power he held, the boy intentionally broke a jar, and one of his servants took the beating that the boy himself deserved.

And, really, that is the way the world operates. The powerless often take the punishment which the powerful deserve. The CEO walks off with millions while the employees of the bankrupt company walk away empty-handed. But that is not the way the kingdom of God operates. The cross turns our understanding of life upside down. The emperor, or the CEO of the universe, takes the punishment that should have been ours. Can we get your minds around that? This is the gospel, the good news we celebrate this night. On the cross of Calvary, Christ took our sins upon himself.

Some people are offended by that. Someday tell people that you are a follower of a 33-year-old idealist who so offended society that society put him in prison and executed him. People probably will say, "Are you sure you want to advertise that? Why not focus on the positive?" It's a terrible growth strategy for the church, all that morbid suffering and bleeding and dying.

The cross reminds us we cannot — should not — always avoid the painful and hard in search of the pleasant and easy. No athlete becomes great without strenuous workouts. No saint is canonized without suffering. Eleanor Roosevelt said: "Do one thing every day that scares you. Those small things that make us uncomfortable help us build courage to do the work we do."

The Bible's word for cross, *stauros*, is almost identical in meaning to the "thorn in the flesh" that Paul said afflicted him (2 Corinthians 12:7). To be afflicted with a problem not of your own making is to carry your own cross of suffering.

Beyond suffering, the cross represents the shame of our brokenness. Death by crucifixion was Rome's way of humiliating as well as torturing the victim. Onlookers were expected to mock for this was lynch-mob entertainment, a ritualized extermination.

And yet this cross, this symbol of suffering and shame, we lift high as the promise of God's love, God's power.

In my favorite liturgy is an offertory with these last lines:

God, whose joy is to transform
In his image we are born.
Let the Easter life begin.
His tomb, a womb — life again.

You might think the 'tomb is a womb' line is pretty creepy. Might as well throw in rhymes about "gloom and doom." Yes, Christ's tomb is the womb for his resurrection life. Crosses and tombs are not things of beauty. But the cross carries God's promise of new life. Remember that every cross is pointed up toward heaven.

At least we don't have the problem of one famous mega church in California. When the church was built a half century ago the pastor asked that no cross be seen anywhere. "We don't want anyone to think about weakness or failure," he said.

Some Christians want us to be a Dale Carnegie meeting, not a church. A motivational rally, not a community of redemption and sacrifice. The most precious symbol of the church is the cross. Mark this down. Our faith was born in failure, rejection and despair. If you've ever failed at something, if you've ever been rejected by somebody, if you've ever despaired over the condition of the world, or of the condition of someone you love, or if you have ever despaired over your own life and what you have made of it — you can take heart in this. God has been where you are. The cross is the symbol of hatred and scorn and bitterness and fear and rejection and hurt and despair. But the cross is not the last word on these emotions. The empty tomb is God's last victorious word on our lives. But Easter's conquest would not have been possible without Good Friday's cross. The tomb is the womb for new life.

Philippians 2: 5-11 are the verses that best exemplify who Jesus is and why he came to us. What is the key message in these verses? That Jesus, though having equality with God, humbled himself and took the form of a bond servant, or slave. Jesus didn't just come as an ordinary man. He humbled himself to the point of being a slave for us. Nothing was beneath him, not even his humiliation and death, if it would save us. There is an old adage — people try to fix problems with duct tape and WD-40®; God did it with nails.

This is why we are here this night. To focus on Christ's cross. Not to focus on our dreams and ambitions, but to focus on God's dreams and God's ambitions for us in light of what Christ has done for us. By his wounds, says the prophet, we are healed.

Many years ago, my church hired our church secretary's husband to work for the church for a few months. Paul had managed Big Lot® stores, and he was a wheeler and dealer. He was between jobs, and we asked him to come in and make the church more efficient — repair broken things, make us energy efficient and work with vendors of our school and church to get the best deals he could.

It was during this time I was making some TV programs for the synod. We needed to film a few seconds of someone carrying a cross. Paul agreed. One afternoon he dressed up in what looked like a first century robe and went into a ravine near the church. There, as cars drove past and passengers stared at him, Paul carried the cross up and down for the camera. You couldn't see his face on camera, but we drew a crowd, and Paul knew that people were looking at *him*.

When he finally left our employment to work in a permanent job Paul said that afternoon of filming changed him. He could no longer use vulgar language at work or join in games that demeaned people or make deals so sharp they hurt the other guy. He would say, "I have to watch myself. I'm the one who carried Jesus' cross."

From baptism's oil to this night's smear of ashes, we all carry the cross of Christ.

Amen.

A Study Guide For God's Test

In the Genesis reading today, Adam was about to be sent into the wilderness. In the gospel, Jesus was *in* the wilderness. Both men were struggling. Both were dealing with the most fundamental sins facing the world. And they both face temptations.

To understand temptation let's remember that the word the Bible uses for temptation literally means to test. It is the word used in the story of God testing Abraham when he told Abraham to sacrifice his son Isaac to prove that God was more important to him than his son. Temptation doesn't mean to seduce into doing evil — temptation means God is pushing you to see what you're made of. Temptations are meant to strengthen us like iron ore in a hot fire is strengthened and shaped as steel — you're meant to come out of temptations better and stronger than before. It's not wrong to be tested — even Jesus was tempted. It's only wrong to fail the test.

In Genesis, the temptation is simple and broad — eat the forbidden fruit and you become like God. We call it original sin and it's the most basic sin of all — self-centeredness — thinking the world revolves around you or me.

Today's gospel is more subtle in speaking of temptations. Jesus has just been baptized and heard God's voice, "This is my Son, with whom I am well pleased." After that high point of his life, Jesus goes off into the wilderness on a retreat. This becomes a low point in his life as Satan appears. The fascinating thing is that these temptations he dangled before Jesus were as modern as the latest iPhone. They were the most basic sins that face people. When you ask people, "When you think of a sin, what comes to mind?" — most people will talk about sex or perhaps racism or gluttony. Yet Jesus seldom spoke of those things. For Jesus there are three fundamental sins and all stem from Adam's original sin of self-centeredness. Those three sins are behind the three temptations Jesus faced in the wilderness. And they are the sins plaguing our nation today and leaving us in the wilderness.

The first temptation and the first sin — greed. In today's gospel, it is expressed as comfort. The devil tempted Jesus to make stones into loaves of bread. It's the temptation for creaturely comforts — beyond just food, it is wealth, mansions, opulence, a fat life where all your needs are exceeded. Jesus rejected this. "One does not live for bread alone," he says. Live to become close to God.

The second sin was for fame. How many X (formerly Twitter) followers can you muster? For Jesus, the temptation was to jump from the pinnacle of the temple, letting God's angels catch him. The pinnacle of the temple could mean one of two things. It might mean the edge of the plateau on which the temple was built. Today's Wailing Wall is the supporting wall of that plateau and is the most famous remnant of that temple compound. This plateau overlooked the Kedron Valley. To leap from the edge of the plateau into the valley was a 450-foot drop. Or this pinnacle of the temple could mean a small perch on top of the temple's roof. Every morning before dawn a trumpeter would climb to this perch and at dawn dramatically blow his trumpet telling people it was time to wake up and pray. The temple was about fourteen stories high so anyone jumping from here would also need angels to catch him to save him from death. This second temptation is to do something glamorous, something showy, something to make you famous. It's the temptation for the big, the splashy, for something that will have everyone talking and tweeting. You have angels catch you in midair as you jump from the great temple, and you'll have your face on the cover of *Time* magazine. But

Jesus rejected this quest for fame. "Do not put the Lord your God to the test."

The third sin, the third temptation, is for power. It may be the worst sin of all. Worship the devil and you can have all the kingdoms of the world. Then you can get rid of those people you don't like. And you can have all the money you want.

America is in the wilderness right now struggling with these same temptations, succumbing to these same sins. You see it so clearly in the people who come from Washington, DC. The purpose of so many politicians is to gain power and wealth and airtime. Serve in government in Washington for a few years or decades and you can become a lobbyist to make millions of dollars influence peddling. How can a community organizer in Chicago become a senator and then president earning a total $3.7 million in salary over his twelve years in Washington — how can he now be worth over $70 million and own four estates in Martha's Vineyard, Washington, Chicago, and the former Magnum PI TV show estate in Hawaii — four estates together worth $31 million? You don't get such money from a government salary.

How can a drug-addicted son of a president, a loser with no artistic experience, sell for millions of dollars abstract paintings which he supposedly painted himself, to people we are not allowed to know, so we are not allowed to know the quid pro quo involved?

How is the former Speaker of the House allowed to tell her stock-trader husband about upcoming legislation before other market movers know, so that now they are worth $125 million?

How could a 34-year-old congressman from Long Island lie about everything on his resume during the campaign, and after being elected and caught in his lies, merely says, "Sometimes everyone does something stupid."

And this doesn't even mention Washington's most recent crime family dominating the headlines of honest news channels. A president who resembled King Lear, demented but demanding loyalty; crazed King Lear, but without the ultimate remorse and repentance.

This nation is falling just as the Roman Empire fell and for the same reasons — lust for power, wealth, and fame by our leaders!

Do you face similar temptations? How do we deal with temptations?

The Bible gives several guidelines. Think of these as a study guide for God's temptation test.

First be honest. Be honest with yourself and with God. Psalm 51 says of people praying to God: "You desire truth from deep within me; therefore, teach me wisdom in my inmost heart. Create in me a clean heart, O Lord, and renew a right spirit within me." Adam and Eve's problem was not simply that they ate the forbidden fruit; it's that they rationalized and evaded God. Jesus, on the other hand, faced his temptations squarely and named them and rejected them. He told Satan where to go. A real mark of health and hope is to say, "I have a problem with this", whether the problem is pride or greed or lust or depression or jealousy. Simply be honest. The Alcoholic Anonymous model is so wise — When an AA member wants a drink, he calls his sponsor and says, "I need to talk." Then with honesty and openness the late-night drink they share is coffee.

The second way to handle temptation — hang around joyful, positive people. That's what each congregation should be. Be careful about who you let into your life. Satan loves to use angry, sour, bitter, slandering people around us to bring turmoil and confusion to our communities. I pray and work constantly for a sweet spirit in myself and in this church. It's much easier to overcome life's problems and temptations when we're surrounded by upright, upbeat people. 1 Corinthians 15:33 says, "Do not be misled; bad company corrupts good character."

Third, renew your mind. I use music and inspirational reading and art and even movies to renew my mind and spirit. They steer me away from temptations. It's easier for me to try to be upright and brave after I've watched *To Kill A Mockingbird* or read Psalm 23. Dwell on what is good and not what is evil. Romans 12:2 says, "Do not conform any longer to the pattern of this world but be transformed by the renewing of your mind. Then you will be able to test and approve what God's will is; his good, pleasing and perfect will." And remember that great passage from Philippians: "Beloved, whatever is true. Whatever is honorable, whatever is just, whatever is pure, whatever is pleasing, whatever is commendable, if there is any excellence and if there is anything worthy of praise, think about *these* things… and the God of peace will be with you" (4:8).

Fourth, leave the past in the past. Once you've confessed your sins to God, the Lord casts them as far as the east is from the west. Sometimes our friends, family, and even other Christians love to bring up our troubled past because it makes them feel more in control or feel better about their own failures. To avoid the temptation for bitterness or guilt claim divine amnesia. Isaiah 43 says, "Forget the former things; do not dwell on the past. See, I am doing a new thing! Now it springs up; do you not perceive it? I am making a way in the desert and streams in the wasteland." It's divine amnesia.

Fifth, study and memorize scripture. That's what Jesus did in the wilderness. He quoted the Bible back at Satan. John 15:3 says, "You are already clean because of the *word* I have spoken to you." *Studying* the Bible improves your attitude. It helps place you inside God's great story rather than stuck in the world's sick story. Study gives you power to avoid temptation and sin. The more you understand the promises of God, the more confident you will be in your ability to overcome temptation. Find and memorize passages that deal with your situation and repeat them until you believe them in your spirit.

And last — elect honest political leaders who seek to serve others and not themselves.

In a way Satan's temptations of Jesus in the wilderness are like what the serpent said to Adam and Eve — "Eat this and be like God." Satan told Jesus, "You deserve better than what God has given you." Why should God's son be hungry? Why shouldn't angels keep you safe and give you honor? Why shouldn't you be in charge of everything? Aren't you God's son?

Notice, that's what Satan says several times. "If you are the Son of God…" Adam and Eve fell because they forgot who they were — forgot they were children of God and tried to be God herself. Jesus did *not* fall because he knew what *Son of God* meant. God's Son did not use magic. God's Son didn't seek special protection or political power. The Son of God did not rise out of his humanity into glory, but sank into humanity even when he is famished, even when he is taunted by Satan himself. God's Son was one who could listen to every good reason to make himself center of the universe and God the Father's rival, and yet remains God's child instead.

This wasn't just a story about Jesus' identity, was it? How often we are tempted to think we deserve bigger and better than what we have. That devilish voice in our heads says, "You're a child of God. Can't you do whatever you need to do to be richer, more powerful, more famous?" That's when we need to say what Jesus once said — "Get behind me Satan." Scram, temptation.

If you can do that you can help keep this nation from falling. If you can resist temptation and hold others accountable to resist temptation you can help lead this nation out of the wilderness. And if you can do that then in time you are likely to hear another voice in your head, a beautiful voice, saying, "This is my beloved child in whom I am well pleased."

Amen.

You Only Live Twice

Nicodemus was probably an old man when he came to Jesus. The Bible says he was a leader of the Jews and of the Pharisees, and only gray beards were such leaders. He was confronted with living in a body that was not as vigorous as it once was. He was also conscious of dreams that would never be fulfilled. It's not easy to age, is it? Even middle age can be disconcerting.

Those of us who are older remember life sixty years ago. Back then closets were for clothes, not for "coming out of". Fast food was what we ate on Fridays during Lent. "Going like sixty" meant moving fast, not crawling in the right lane. There was no computer dating, dual careers, house husbands or iPads. Letter groupings such as DEI, DNA or ELCA would have been lovers' initials carved on a tree. Aging is not easy. As one man put it, "I still have something on the ball, but I'm less interested in bouncing it."

Nicodemus was confronted with aging. He had lived a good life and was respected in the community. But like most people he wanted to turn the clock back. So, imagine how astonished he was when Jesus said to him, "No one can see the kingdom of God without being born from above." Flabbergasted, Nicodemus said to him, "How can anyone be born after having grown old? Can one enter a second time into the mother's womb and be born?" Jesus answered, "Truly I say to you, unless one is born of water and the Spirit, he cannot enter the kingdom of God."

Jesus was giving Nicodemus the opportunity to be young twice. The first time he was young in years. The second time he was be young spiritually.

In the days of Jesus, the Roman Empire had recently developed a new calendar, the Julian calendar. Unfortunately, it wasn't very accurate and for centuries people had to subtract a few days every decade or so. Finally, in 1582 a new calendar was introduced to better match the true length of the year. But people were reluctant to change, and many protested losing several days. The cry of this opposition was "Give us back our days".

Even Jesus could not give Nicodemus back his days — he could not make him chronologically young again — but he could make his days richer, more satisfying, more fulfilling. He could be young twice.

Now, contrast Nicodemus' fearful, confused reaction to Jesus' offer with Abraham's reaction to God's call. Abraham was an old man when God came to him — if you consider 75 years of age to be old. It's not nearly as old as it used to be considering that people of that age run marathons, work fulltime jobs, and blast off into space. And that's the point, isn't it. Aging does not have to mean trauma and tragedy. A lot has to do with attitude. You're as young as you feel.

Remember, Abraham was not some poor wanderer living in a tent when he heard God's voice. Ur, his hometown, was a wealthy city at the height of power and influence. God came to Abraham at Ur and said, "Go from your country and your kindred and your father's house to the land that I will show you. I will make of you a great nation, and I will bless you, and make your name great, so that you will be a blessing. I will bless those who bless you, and the one who curses you I will curse; and by you all the families of the earth will be blessed." So, Abraham went. Into the unknown, without a job or allies beyond family and friends, he went to a strange land. And in that going — *he became young again.*

You see, you can live twice. Once when you're born, and the second time when you obey God's voice, and head into whatever new direction God takes you. That's when you are born spiritually. And that can happen at any age.

In the Nicodemus story Jesus' actual words were, "You must be born from above." Sometimes Christians have translated that as "You must be born again." Some Christians use an emotional born-again experience as an adult as the litmus test of true faith. "If you can't tell others a dramatic, born-again experience, then you're not a true Christian." But Christ is talking about a spiritual rebirth, not an emotional one, and that "born from above" gift of the Spirit is what we expect at baptism, including the baptism of infants.

Yet, let's not discount the "born again" experience of adulthood. Some people have genuine religious conversion as adults that wake them to a whole new way of seeing reality. That's what Abraham had; it's what Moses had at the burning bush. It's what Augustine had in his garden when he heard a voice say, "Take up and read", and he picked up the nearest book — a Bible — and read the exact criticism of his wild lifestyle that made him renounce immorality. And this religious conversion is what Jesus offered Nicodemus but which, sadly, old, frightened Nicodemus declined.

What about those of us who were "born from above" at Baptism but don't have a specific "born again" experience as adults? We can have a *gradual* spiritual awakening. We may not be able to recount a specific time, but in our inner struggles we find a purpose, a direction, something to live for. We are able to escape the prison of self-absorption. We have more energy because our attitude is more positive, more hopeful. We age better because we do not isolate ourselves in depression and despair. We are involved in a church. We are involved with people. We're driven by dreams, and we sleep well at night without guilt. We live openly and joyfully. In short, we do all the things that are part of staying young right through the twilight of our years. You know people like that, don't you? Of course you do. Many of them are right here in our church.

These are people who know what it is to turn their lives over to God — to go where God leads them. This is what it means to be born both chronologically and spiritually. It is to yield our lives to the Divine.

And that means not always knowing where you're going in life. Notice in this Gospel lesson, Jesus says, "The wind blows where it chooses, and you hear the sound of it, but you do not know where it comes from or where it goes." In Greek the word for "wind" and the word for "spirit" are the same. When God's Spirit blows into you, you cannot predict what God has in mind for you. As St. Augustine once said, "One sure sign of the presence of God is that we will be led where we had not planned to go."

Imagine your life is like riding a tandem bicycle. As a child you are on the back seat and your parents are in the front, making the decisions for your life's direction and providing most of the pedal power. Life is loving but too serene. As an adult you leave your parents behind, and you move into the front seat. You go where you want and under your own power. Your trip is predictable but often boring. But if you have faith, you gradually sense someone else is sitting behind you now, whispering directions and adding encouragement and energy to the pedaling. The voice from behind suggests new destinations, often more scenic or unexpected. Then, in time, the wind blows. Now you recognize you are on the back seat of the bike and this voice from behind is the God who now is in charge and on the front seat. With God leading, you ride up mountains and through rocky places, often at breakneck speeds. You swallow hard and hang on!

You ask God where you are going and only hear a faint laughter. But you learn to trust. Life is no longer boring but an adventure. When you whisper that you're scared, he leans back so he is closer.

He takes you to people and places with gifts you need, gifts of healing, acceptance, talent and joy. Then you are off again, the Lord and you.

In time you realize you value too much the gifts you have been given. The voice in front says, "Give some gifts away;

they're extra baggage, too much weight." So, you do, to the people you meet, and you find in the giving you receive, and your burden is light.

You do not trust him, at first, in control of your life. You fear he will wreck you. But he knows the journey and he knows what a bike can do, how to make it bend to take sharp turns. He knows how to jump high rocks, how to fly past scary passages, how to shift gears for uphill climbs.

You learn to be still and pedal in the strangest places and you enjoy the view and the cool breeze with your wonderful companion, Jesus Christ. And when you think you just can't do it anymore, He just smiles and says… "Pedal!"

Are you ready to leap onto God's bicycle? Do you want to be young again spiritually, regardless of your age? You can live twice. You do it when you whisper to God, "Lord, lead me wherever *you* want me to go."

Amen.

The Conversation That Never Should Have Happened

Recently a bride asked a baker to make her wedding cake. She asked him to inscribe on top the words from I John 4:18. Verse 18 of chapter 4 of John's first letter reads: "There is no fear in love, but perfect love casts out fear." Unfortunately, the cake decorator did not know the Bible well — he did not know there is a difference between the gospel of John and the first letter of John. And unfortunately, the bride and groom did not see the cake until they came to cut the cake at the reception. There, for all to read, was 4:18 from John's gospel: "You have had five husbands and the man you now have is not your husband."

These last were words Jesus spoke to a woman at noon one day. He met her at the ancient village well in the town of Sychar in Samaria. You can still see the well. There are many reasons this conversation should never have happened. Jesus was regarded as a rabbi and in that land such esteemed men do not speak to women in public. Supreme Court Justice William O. Douglas once visited a country in this part of the world. In his book, *Strange Lands And Friendly People*, he recalled talking with two Muslim women in the desert when the husband of one arrived. The man swore at his wife, hit her with his fist, and knocked her to the ground. After he drove the women off the man came to Douglas to apologize. But he didn't apologize for this behavior. He apologized for his wife's conduct — that she was so forward to talk with a stranger.

Beside women having been forbidden from speaking to strange men in public, this woman was a Samaritan and Jesus was a Jew. Over 700 years before, there had been a religious fight in Israel. In 722 BCE people from what today is Syria conquered northern Israel, including the region of Samaria. Many Israelites were carted off into permanent exile. Many of those who remained intermarried with the invaders and adopted some of their pagan religious practices. Then, in 586 BCE Babylon conquered Judea (the portion of Israel not earlier conquered) and carted off more than a quarter of the population into a seventy-year captivity in Babylon. When their descendants were freed to return, they had a new identity. They were not simply Israelites. They were people who had come from the region of Judea. They were now called Jews. Some people of Samaria came to help these repatriated Jews rebuild the Jerusalem temple but the Jews considered them turncoats and sent them home. Jews saw Samaritans as insolent and sinful and would not let them in the Jerusalem temple; Samaritans saw Jews as arrogant, so they built their own temple thirty miles north of Jerusalem. It was a bitter feud that made the Hatfields and the McCoys look cozy by comparison.

There was another problem Jesus saw when looking at this woman at the well. This woman had been married five times and Jewish law said any woman married more than three times was a prostitute. John's gospel made a point of saying Jesus was at the well at noon. Any self-respecting woman of the village would draw water early in the morning or early in the evening when it was cool. The well was a gathering place for socializing at those times. This woman went in the heat of the day because she was scorned and didn't think she would run into other women there. No wonder Jesus' disciples were shocked when they saw Jesus with her.

How remarkable, then, that Jesus treated this woman with gentleness, kindness, and respect. He called her "*gune*," which is the Greek word for respected lady, like calling her "ma'am." "*Gune*" is also what Jesus called his own mother when she asked him to turn water into wine at a wedding and when he was hanging on the cross. In essence, Jesus forgave this Samaritan woman. He said she could overcome her past. He saw potential where others only saw shame.

Imagine the power of forgiveness to transform a life. I don't know anything more powerful in a human than Christian forgiveness. God wipes the slate clean and offers divine amnesia for the baggage we carry. That word *forgive* comes from the words "give" and "forth" and means a generous handing over of something. When Jesus spoke lovingly to this woman, he not only wiped away a troubled past; he handed her a future. He accepted the cup of water she handed him and in return offered her "living water" — joy and eternal life. He even told her that he was the Messiah. That made her the first person to learn his true identity. The disciples did not know he was God's Son; neither did the wise men. Jesus told this woman first — quite an honor for a shady lady.

Have you ever experienced the power of forgiveness in your life? Forgiveness helps create a bond of trust and respect between people. You both know that together you've succeeded in overcoming a hurtful past. You know how a bone that is broken is strongest at the point of the break when it heals. That's what forgiveness does for the break between humans.

Fifteen years ago, Warsaw, Ohio, was in national news because of a feud between a church and a nearby strip club. Members of New Beginnings Ministries Church would picket outside the Foxhole Club and take pictures of the license plates of the cars visiting. The club owner retaliated by having his show girls in bikinis outside of the church on Sunday mornings. They held signs with Bible quotes about false prophets. This went on for months. Then came a visit from members of JC's Girls based in San Diego. JC's Girls is a ministry reaching out to women trapped in the adult entertainment industry. They bring pizza and small gifts and tell the women of God's love. Two ladies from JC's Girls visited that Ohio church with a plea to replace judgment with mercy. Pastor Craig Gross of

JC's Girls said. "Our motto is: 'You can't blame the dark for being dark, you have to blame the light for not shining on the dark.'" The Warsaw church gave this forgiveness a try. Church members quietly talked with the bikini girls protesting. They prayed together, tears flowed, and lives were changed in both protest lines. (*Christianity Today* September 13, 2010.)

In the musical *The Man of La Mancha*, the crazy knight, Don Quixote, calls Aldonza, the dirty serving wench from the bar, by the name of Dulcinea. Like the word Guna, Dulcinea means "Special Lady." Everyone scoffed at Don Quixote. His scoffers eventually kill him, just as scoffers killed Jesus. But, of course, Don Quixote's respect for her gradually gave Aldonza the self-respect to become Dulcinea. She lived up to her name. Doesn't Jesus give each of us a similar love far beyond what we deserve?

It's utterly remarkable how God can transform people. There is a passage in Luke 7:47 where Jesus forgave a sinful woman and people questioned whether such generous forgiveness was wise. Jesus told them, "Therefore, I tell you, her sins, which are many, have been forgiven, for she loved much; but he who has been forgiven little, loves little." It's so often true — the wilder, more wicked, more wretched we are, the sweeter and more centered in Christ we can become.

In this story it's not just the forgiving that was remarkable. It was the forgetting. Jesus forgot he was thirsty when he started talking with the woman. He forgot the animosity between Jews and Samaritans, the societal difference between rabbis and women, the expectation that he should condemn her sins. And the woman forgot, too. She forgot her water jar. She forgot her reputation as a "fallen woman" and ran back to town to tell others of Jesus — "Come and see.... Can this be the Christ?" She forgot that many of the men she met only wanted to possess her. She forgot in the presence of this strange prophet who spoke with words and eyes of respect. She forgot other people's definitions and he forgot their rules, and that made all the difference.

Forgiveness only works when we can forget, when we can let go of the past. General Oglethorpe, founder of the colony of Georgia, once said to John Wesley, "I never forgive and I never forget." Wesley replied, "Then, sir, I hope you never sin."

Author Corrie ten Boom spoke of forgiving and forgetting. "It was 1947. I had come from Holland to a defeated Germany with the message that God *forgives*. It was the truth they needed most to hear in that bitter, bombed-out land, and I gave them my favorite mental picture. Maybe because the sea is never far from a Hollander's mind, I like to think that's where *forgiven* sins are thrown. "When we confess our sins," I said, "God casts them into the deepest ocean, gone forever. Then God places a sign out there that says, 'No Fishing Allowed '"(Corrie ten Boom, in her book, *Tramp for the Lord, CLC Publications* (Fort Washington, PA 19034) 1974, page 55)

Can we both forgive and forget? Can you forget your own certainty long enough to let a new idea break in? Can we forget that once we were angry? Can you forget that years ago, after confirmation or after some life-wrenching tragedy you said that religion wasn't for you? Can you forget the explanations you had as a child long enough to risk grown-up questions which your disregarded faith could never answer? Can you and I forget our cynicism — our certainty that there is no goodness or hope — in order to look for innocence and caring? Can we forget our bitterness over something from the past in order to hear Jesus' promise that the past does not define us forever?

At the ancient village well in the town of Sychar in what used to be Samaria, Jesus met a woman. There are all kinds of reasons their conversation should never have happened. But they forgot those reasons long enough to forgive. Freed of her past, she became one of the first evangelists. "Can this be the Christ?" she asked. Forget your preconceived ideas. Come and see.

Amen.

Fourth Sunday in Lent

John 9:1-41

To See In A New Way

(Note: Go online and download three images. Two are found as optical illusions — Young Lady or Old Woman; Goblet or Two Faces; the third is a Maltese Cross. Put these on the sanctuary screen or print them in the bulletin.)

Let's take a test. In this picture what do you see? *(Young Lady/ Old Woman)*

Yes, a woman. But is it a fashionable young lady in furs and feathers looking away? Or is it a tired old lady looking down?

And what about this picture — what do you see? *(Goblet/ Two Faces)* Many people see a goblet being poured. Tilt it to the left and you can see two faces.

We all see things differently. But notice something. How did you feel when you recognized the second interpretation of each picture? Isn't that "Ah-ha" moment priceless? To be flooded with new insight, a refreshing new way to see reality, is to be given a second childhood.

It is to see in a new way.

Consider this cross. Have you ever seen the Maltese Cross before? Veterans of World War II in Europe or people who know their military history would recognize it as the Iron Cross, the emblem of the German military, the mark of the old enemy. But see that cross in a new way. It originated seven hundred years ago as the emblem of a brotherhood of knights in the Holy Land. The Knights Hospitaler were a curious mixture of monks and military knights of noble birth. Both wore cloaks with this eight- pointed cross. Their purpose was simple. Palestine, at that time the name for Israel, was controlled by Arab Muslims. Because Christian pilgrims feared for their safety on their way to Jerusalem, the Knights Hospitaler gave them safe convoy. They also gave those pilgrims food and shelter, hospitality and even hospitals. Eventually after the crusades failed all Christians were forced from the Holy Land and this religious order resettled on the island of Malta. Hence their cross is called the Maltese Cross.

But the interesting thing is what those Knights Hospitaler — those hospitality knights — saw when they looked at this cross. They recognized the futility and bloody failure of the crusades and were convinced there was a better way of promoting the faith than taking up the sword against nonbelievers. The life of humble service became their goal. And so, they developed the eight-pointed Maltese Cross to represent the eight beatitudes. Those were the qualities they wanted. The eight points of the cross are for humility, mercy, willingness to mourn, purity of heart, righteousness, peacemaker, poverty in spirit, and willingness to be persecuted. The feared Iron Cross is originally the Beatitudes Cross.

To see things in a new way.

That's what today's gospel is all about. Our scripture today is about a man who was healed from blindness, but it is much more than that. It is about people who are not only physically blind, but those who are morally and spiritually blind as well. This is the longest story in the gospels before Maundy Thursday. Yet only verses 6 and 7 of this gospel describe healing actions. The other 39 verses are about people's hurtful reactions.

The story of the hymn, "Amazing Grace" helps explain this gospel story. The hymn was written by an English pastor named John Newton who experienced a dramatic conversion. In his early adult years, he was a slave trader involved in the selling of people. When Jesus came into his life John Newton repented his sinfulness and turned his life around.

"Amazing Grace, how sweet the sound that saved a wretch like me" is John Newton's life story. As Newton read this ninth chapter of John's gospel, he saw himself reflected in the experience of the man whose eyes were opened. When the formerly blind man was asked the source of his healing, he responded with the words Newton used in his hymn, "I once was blind, but now I see." Though John Newton was not physically blind, he was morally and spiritually blind. This is the key to understanding today's gospel for Jesus taught us that there were many ways that we can be blind.

In this gospel the disciples of Jesus were blind. As they walked with Jesus through Jerusalem they came upon a blind man, and then proceeded to talk about him as if he wasn't even there! They reflected an insensitive mindset to those with limitations and disabilities. You and I have seen an amazing change take place in our society in recent decades regarding to the rights of the disabled — thank God. The physically and mentally challenged were being respected and brought into the mainstream of society. But the disciples spoke of the blind man as if he wasn't there and then they had the audacity to speculate on the cause of his blindness. They wondered, "Is he blind because of something he did or blind because of something his parents did?" In biblical times, conventional wisdom held that if you had a disability, it was the result of sin. The man blind from birth presented a perplexing problem for the disciples. How could he have sinned before he was born? Or, had his parents done something so awful that the result would be a child born blind? For the disciples, new sight meant realizing there are some problems in life for which no one is to blame — not yourself, not your parents, not your society. The blame game, pointing fingers, gives the illusion of dealing with a problem but solves nothing. For the disciples, new sight meant empathy, meant allowing your heart to break for someone, meant gazing deeply into a tragedy without forcing a shallow answer.

The second person needing new sight is the blind man himself.

But it wasn't eyesight he needed; it was insight. For the man born blind new sight meant being open to the miraculous power of Christ. Jesus understood the man's blindness to be an opportunity for healing and teaching. With the eyesight came faith and insight. Sadly, part of the insight was that following

Jesus would be costly. He would be scorned and thrown out of town by the religious authorities for not fitting in. With incredible irony, he could see, but what he saw was painful — that his old, pat understandings of religion and society didn't work anymore. He was way out of his comfort zone. He must go to Christ to find comfort.

Jesus gave the blind man his sight and there should have been joy, but the Pharisees threw a wet blanket over everything. *They were the third people who needed new sight for they were blinded by cynicism and resentment.*

Cynicism — verse 18 said some in the crowd believed the blind man never was blind. Think about it — the only way a blind man could support himself in those days was by begging and this pool of Siloam was a popular spot for begging. This man with his cup had probably been there for years but the Pharisees apparently were blind to him. But now they asked his parents, "Is this your son who you *say* was born blind?" These Pharisees were cynical and when you are cynical you condemn yourself to bitterness. Cynicism is corrosive. Cynicism masquerades as wisdom, but it is the farthest thing from it, because the cynic never learns anything. The cynic is blinded by hurt or disappointment or anger and rejects the world for fear of further hurts. Or, as H.L. Mencken said somewhat cynically, "A cynic is a man who, when he smells flowers, looks around for a coffin."

The Pharisees around the blind man were cynics. They also were jealous. They couldn't see anything new or good for they begrudged Jesus' popularity. This healing of the blind man had taken place on the Sabbath, the day of rest, and some of the Pharisees were bent out of shape because Jesus had "worked" on the Sabbath by healing someone. The Pharisees confronted the formerly blind man. They rode him hard, telling him that he must be a sinner, that his sin caused him to be born blind. But the young man had gumption. He answered with those words that became the basis for "Amazing Grace." He said that he didn't know if he was a sinner or not, he just knew that he once was blind, but now he could see. He didn't know much, but he knew that only a man sent from God could open the eyes of a man born blind! Well, this wasn't the answer the Pharisees had been looking for, so they drove the man right out of the community. The Pharisees were really "Fear-i-sees".

This is the moment when the entire story came together. Jesus came to the man born blind when he was all alone and asked him, "Do you believe in the Son of man?" "And who is he sir?" he asked. "Tell me, so that I might believe in him." "You have seen him," said Jesus, "and the one speaking with you is he." With these words of love, the young man worshiped Jesus and told him that he did believe. The young man was now whole in body and spirit. Finally, he saw with his heart as well as his eyes.

The blind man was the most exciting character in this gospel. He was not the object of pity; he was the hero. This man was like the blind men you read about in the plays of Shakespeare or of the ancient Greeks — he was the wisest person around. Lacking eyesight he had developed keen insight. Notice, he began by hearing Jesus called "rabbi." Then, in verse 17 he promoted Jesus by calling him a prophet. By the end of the gospel, he confessed that Jesus was the Son of Man and worshiped him. He even had the self-confidence of in-your-face humor. To the Pharisees he said, "Look (no pun intended); do you also want to be his disciples?" This man who has been compliant, obedient to Jesus, now showed the best attitude of all toward life. He celebrated. Oh, he was driven out of the temple but that simply liberated him to find Christ, to find a new life. He was free — free of critics, condemners, and cynics.

Over a century ago, the poet John Keats wrote an ode to the world's first great poet, the blind Homer. Twenty-six hundred years ago Homer wrote *The Iliad* and *The Odyssey*. Keats penned these lines:

> *There's a budding morrow in midnight*
> *There is triple sight in blindness keen.*

Keats could have been writing about this blind man who could see where others overlooked; who could do while others questioned; who could trust when others scorned.

Finally, Jesus said, "I have come into the world so that those who are blind might see and that those who have sight might become blind." He was saying that when we think we have all the answers, when we think we know what is right for ourselves as well for others, it's then that we truly are blind. Sight has to do with the mind and the heart as well as the eyes. It means to see in a new way all that you had missed before. It means to be open to God's mystery. It means to leave behind comfortable old stereotypes.

In my little hometown there was a man named Milo. Milo was a character. He was the town drunk, a little mentally challenged, and earned a living shoveling walks and mowing grass. As children, we were scared of him, made fun of him, and stayed away from him. Then we heard a story — Milo used to work for the Cincinnati Reds. He knew our heroes Frank Robinson and Vida Pinson on a first-name basis. As seven- and eight-year-olds my friends and I dared each other to talk to the frightening Milo to see if the story was true. Finally, the oldest of us, Albert, ramped up his courage and approached him one day when he was cutting a lawn down the street. It turned out that he didn't bite, he was just terribly shy and ashamed. And Milo knew more about baseball than any person alive. He was a walking encyclopedia. After that, if we kids wanted to know anything about baseball, we just tracked down old Milo and asked. Shyly, happily he would help. And we counted him as a fascinating friend.

To see in a new way.

I've always loved how Thornton Wilder in his play "Our Town" made the appeal poetically. In sleepy Grover's Corners, Vermont, young Emily had died. In heaven she begged for the chance to relive just one day of her life. She was granted the wish to return for her twelfth birthday. She was thrilled. She couldn't be heard or seen but she could see and hear. But oh, what she saw. Parents who looked so young but who seemed to sleepwalk through life, not seeing, sensing, or celebrating the gift of each day. Dismayed, Emily asked, "Do any human beings ever realize life while they live it — every minute?" The stage manager quietly replied, "Saints and poets, maybe."

Don't you imagine that this man that Jesus healed had that same excitement about life? That's what happens to us when the scales fall from our eyes — when we swap *our* eyes for the eyes of Christ. We get excited! I'm always amused when I meet a new convert to Christ. They are invariably far more enthusiastic about their faith than those of us who have been believers most of our lives. Why? Because they are seeing the world in a new way.

We began with several questions. Let me end with some more.

Have you wept at anything this past year?

Does your heart beat faster at the sight of beauty?

Do you really listen when others speak to you or are you just waiting for your turn to speak?

Have you recently read some poetry or of some scientific discovery and said, "Wow!"?

Is there anyone you know in whose place, if one of you had to suffer great pain, you would volunteer yourself?

If the answers to those questions are "No", you are probably dead. If consistently it is "Yes", then you, too, are being given the gift of sight.

Amen.

Fifth Sunday of Lent

Ezekiel 37:12-14, John 11:1-45

Dancing With Death

(*For this service show a Celtic cross on the screen or in the bulletin.*)

For six years death has hung over the world. Covid-19 killed seven million people. More than a quarter million people have been killed in the Russia-Ukraine war. The Hamas massacre of Israelis and Israel's revenge is filling thousands of more graves.

Do you think of death often? Do you think of your own death?

Even when facing death at a ripe, old age we are like many Christians — we have a love/hate relationship with death. We have a spiritual schizophrenia about the subject. We dance around the fatal phantom. On the one hand, we regard it as the great enemy — one that interrupts our lives and our relationships. It is the grim reaper — the awful specter that hangs over our lives. We use euphemisms to help us avoid confronting the subject directly. We say *she passed away*, or *he's no longer with us*. We may say *he checked out*, anything except, "He died."

At the same time that we avoid talking about death, we also make the case that we believe death is the Christian's friend. When someone dies, we might say, "She's gone home to be with Jesus." What could be better than that? "He's gone to his eternal rest." No more pain. No more tears. Only a world of eternal bliss.

In a few weeks it will be Easter Sunday, and the church will be filled with happy faces singing "He lives! He lives! Grave where is thy victory? Death, where is thy sting?" So, which is it? Should we look forward to death or should we cling stubbornly to life? The answer is, *Yes*.

In our lesson from Ezekiel, the Lord spoke to people who see no hope after death. God says: "O my people, I am going to open your graves and bring you up from them . . . Then you, my people, will know that I am the Lord . . . I will put my Spirit in you, and you will live." To the reader of the Hebrew Bible, this was good news. There is no highly developed doctrine of life after death in the Old Testament. Death *was* the ultimate enemy. The reward for a righteous life was a long life and maybe children to carry on your name. So, it was awesome news to hear that, one day, graves would be opened, and that the Spirit of God would breathe life into the dead and welcome them to new life.

The raising of Lazarus was an example of hope where there was no hope. He was a friend of Jesus. His sisters, Mary and Martha, could not understand why Christ didn't hustle to help when he heard that Lazarus was near death. Death was the enemy. Didn't he care that their brother was dying?

> Mary and Martha could not foresee that Jesus had greater plans in mind for their brother. He would welcome Lazarus from the tomb and celebrate. And Jesus would show all of them they no longer need fear death — for he was the Lord of life and of death. Jesus waited four days to come to Lazarus' tomb because it was a Jewish superstition that a soul hung over the dead body for three days trying to reenter it. By day four, the body was officially dead, and the face had begun to decay. Jesus had waited four days to come to show that he was offering a resurrection, not a resuscitation.

So, again, how should we feel about death? Should we ignore it, deny it, mask it, or should we embrace it, rejoice in it, look forward to it?

A famous Christian cross gives us a clue. The dominant feature of the Celtic Cross is the circle. It is unending, representing the eternal. It was created in the face of great death. What had died was civilization itself, and Christianity seemed on the brink. In the fifth century the Roman Empire had fallen and in the British Isles the Christian subjects of the old empire were petrified. Barbarians had invaded and the Christianized Britons, led according to some by King Arthur, were forced to withdraw west to the rugged mountains of Wales. Would their faith be overwhelmed as their culture had been? Their response to impending doom was improbable faith. They sent missionaries to spread their death-defying faith. Among them, Saint Patrick went to Ireland and Saint Columba to Scotland. It was missionaries to these Celtic lands who created the Celtic Cross to show their confidence that God is unending.

As Christians we trust that death, this final enemy, has been defeated and we will live forever. Does that mean we will escape death? No! We're talking about life eternal, not life immortal.

Immortal means something invisible in you never dies. The body dies, the soul doesn't; the body is bad and expendable while the soul dances on untouched. But that is not what the Bible says. The Bible says when you die you die — period. But then the Bible speaks of resurrection. We don't escape death, we defy it by being reborn, given a new body. Saint Paul even said we would be recognizable in the next life: "Now I know in part; then I shall know fully, even as I am fully known" (1 Corinthians 13:12). We enter heaven as a new and improved model of ourselves as human — sensitive, wise, and joyous.

That Celtic Cross has this feeling of defiance of death. While the circle in the center makes it the cross of the eternal, the heavy construction of the cross makes it the cross of the earthy. This is the only religious cross designed originally not to be etched on a wall, worn around the neck, stitched onto clothing, or carried in a procession, but rather to be planted in the ground. These crosses weren't made from gold, silver, or polished wood but from rough stone. The first Celtic Crosses were made in Ireland, Scotland, and Wales, the land of the Celts. They were each carved from a single block of stone. Many still survive after 1,500 years. They are a reminder that God comes to us in humble, earthy things and people.

God comes to us in the present. "The eternal now" is how one theologian put it. "God's eternal today" another said. Jesus put it more profoundly. After Lazarus died, Jesus asked his sister Martha if she believed he would rise again and she replies with a sigh of resignation: "Yes, I know he will rise again in the resurrection on the last day." And Jesus said, "*I am* the resurrection." 'You experience resurrected life whenever you're in my presence.'

God loves the earthy, the here and now. When Jesus heard that his friend was dead, he didn't mouth pious platitudes about what a release death was and the sweet by-and-by of heaven — he cried and then raised a smelly Lazarus. Jesus welcomed him back to life and gave him a few more years of eating food, hugging his sisters and telling stories of life after death. God loves the earthy. Jesus was born in a smelly barn attended to by third shift shepherds and then went on to wander the hills as an adult, often accused of being a wino and a chowhound. God loves the earthy. When God made Adam and Eve, God did it by slapping some mud together and breathing into it the breath of life. That's why we don't say "We have a body" but "we *are* a body" — The flesh and soul are as inextricably part of each other as are the wood and flames of a bonfire.

Which means exactly this: the best answer to the fear of death is to live life now with enthusiasm. Enthusiasm — the word literally means "with God's spirit in us." If you want to meet God, don't wait for the next life. Don't even think you can only meet the almighty in a church worship. Go to where life is earthy, to where people are struggling to deal with their daily problems. Go to where people in the muck of life are asking for God's help. Go to where the eternal and the earthy embrace.

Ever wondered how you would deal with life with a debilitating illness? One answer comes in the example of a woman named Zoe Koplowitz.

For fifteen years, Zoe Koplowitz had let multiple sclerosis rule her life. For those fifteen years after she was diagnosed, Zoe didn't push herself much physically. She was afraid of the advance of the disease.

But then one day she got angry. She decided to fight this illness that had so controlled her life. She asked God to help her master her disease. And that's when Zoe Koplowitz made up her mind to participate in the New York City Marathon. The marathon, of course, is a 26-mile event that attracts some of the best runners in the world. Friends joked that Zoe, a full-figured, dark-haired woman who walks with two canes, might easily be mistaken for Grete Waitz, the thin, blond, Norwegian runner who had won eight of the New York City Marathons. Someone even gave Zoe a shawl with the words, "I'm not Grete" embroidered into it.

That year, 1988, Grete Waitz won her ninth New York City Marathon, with a time of 2 hours and 25 minutes. Zoe came struggling in late that night after almost twenty hours of walking. She was dead last, but not dead. For the next five years, Zoe participated in the marathon.

In 1993, Grete and Zoe met at a dinner in Grete's honor. The famed marathon runner was in awe of the woman who pushed herself to compete despite her disabilities. Trying to understand Zoe's motivation, Grete asked, "Who is waiting for you at the finish line?" As a world-renowned runner, Grete was usually greeted by flocks of news reporters and crowds of cheering fans. Zoe replied that no one was waiting for her; by the time she finished the race, everyone else had gone home. That day, Grete Waitz promised that she would be at the finish line next year when Zoe competed in the marathon.

A number of health problems hit Zoe that year, and it took her 28 hours to finish the race. But Grete was waiting right there for her to cross the line. Sadly, someone had stolen a case of finishers' medals, and Grete learned that Zoe would not get a medal for her efforts. So, Grete ran across town to her apartment and asked her husband to give up his own medal that he had just won that day in the marathon. She returned in time to cheer Zoe across the finish line, give her a hug, and drape the medal around her neck.

Zoe Koplowitz has raced in 25 New York Marathons, always finishing last. Every year since they met, Grete Waitz has waited at the finish line for Zoe Koplowitz. The two women also speak at various city schools, where they teach the children a valuable lesson about the winning spirit.

Do you know who's waiting at the finish line for you? The same one who has sustained you all your life — the one who wants to be your friend in everything you do. In the resurrection God, the eternal, and we, the earthy, embrace.

Amen.

The Divine Bow

One of Christianity's most beloved theologians was a tall, courtly man named Krister Stendahl. He was the Dean of Students at Harvard Divinity School. Throughout his ministry in the second half of the twentieth century this gentleman exuded kindness and wisdom. He often said, "Always leave room for 'holy envy'." By that he meant that you should be willing to find elements in the other person's faith that you can admire and wish you could, in some way, reflect in your own faith journey.

Two things people noticed when they first met Stendahl were his height — he stood about 6'5" — and a certain problem with his neck. His neck was stiff. His head was always slightly bowed. He could not look up. When he had to lecture in a tiered classroom where the students were seated on levels above him, that was a problem. But in daily life this persistent bow seemed to shape his character and his relations with others. You always felt he was respectfully bowing in your presence. And his students responded with love and admiration.

In Eastern cultures, the tradition of bowing has always been a part of refined social etiquette. By bowing and bending to each other, members of Eastern cultures show respect and humility before others. There exists a whole language of bowing. Do you bow from the waist or by a nod of the neck? There are bows of different depths, for different purposes — to subtly communicate agreement, disagreement, reverence, gratitude, or respect for those of higher standing.

Western culture has never gone in much for bowing except from stage actors. Is that because western culture is less prone to humility? What drives American culture is an enthusiastic "can-do" spirit that confidently looks at every obstacle as a challenge. Sometimes we even see other people as the challenge. For Americans, the "thumbs-up" signal is the common gesture. Everyone from astronauts to five-year-olds about to swing a bat knows that thumbs-up means pride and confidence. Tackle life with an "A-OK" attitude.

Such a positive, confident outlook is healthy but so is the bow of respect and humility before others. Our challenge is to balance these attitudes — being confident without being "puffed up"; being humble without being a doormat.

Have you ever noticed Jesus' posture during his last days? On Palm Sunday, for instance, the procession into Jerusalem is a type of bowing. Humanity bows to God, kneeling and placing palm branches before Jesus as he rode in. But also, God bows to humanity. Jesus rode into the city on a donkey, his feet only inches above the ground, and his head below many heads in the crowd. The little beast bearing the travel-stained, wandering teacher illustrated Jesus' humble obedience to the divine plan of redemption. This was no sign of power; it was a sign of love at work. The triumphant entry was so modest. Riding horses in a parade was reserved for generals who can look down on their vanquished foes. Jesus was on a donkey, riding low. The divine bow was both to and from God.

Jesus' posture of humility didn't end with Palm Sunday. At the Last Supper Jesus knelt to wash the feet of the disciples. Later that night he knelt again in prayer in the Garden of Gethsemane. When arrested and taken before Pilate he stood silently and made no reply when Pilate asked if he was the rumored king of the Jews. In *Ecco Homo*, the famous painting of the scene by Antonio Ciseri, the Lord was calm, and his head was bowed. Paintings or sketches by Rembrandt, Tintoretto, and Hieronymus Bosch show the same tilt-of-head serenity of Jesus before Pilate.

Now, compare Jesus' Palm Sunday entrance into Jerusalem with the biggest parade that city ever saw. That parade was not Jesus' procession; it was the entrance of German Kaiser Wilhelm II. The year was 1898. Germany had recently built an empire and the kaiser was rich. He wanted to be the first European ruler in 700 years to visit the land of Jesus and in preparation his countrymen built the Lutheran Church of the Redeemer a block from Calvary, the site of Jesus' crucifixion and tomb. They built Christmas Lutheran Church in Bethlehem two blocks from where Jesus was born. They built a palace for the kaiser's party, the Augusta Victoria compound, on the edge of the city. They even widened the city gate, the Jaffe Gate, because the kaiser's oversized carriage could not fit through the ancient gate. The kaiser's entrance parade was huge and noisy — ambassadors from around the world marching, cavalry prancing, a 21-gun salute. The kaiser entered on top of a tall carriage. His head was not bowed. But then, when the parade was over, someone quietly attached a large sign to the gate. It read: "A better man than Wilhelm came through this city's gate. He rode a donkey."

The donkey — the animal of the unpretentious. A bowed head, the sign of respect. For Jesus to ride a donkey was to identify with common people with all their worries and struggles. The word the gospel used for this bowed-head quality of Jesus was humility.

Such humility was not a natural quality for us. Most people would rather be like the kaiser, pre-occupied with our status in the world, about where we stand, what others think of us, how we measure up. Isn't there a little voice within each of us always asking, "How am I doing?" Isn't there a hunger within each of us to be respected by those we think are above us, and to keep a safe distance from those we consider lower than we? There is a humiliation in humility that is uncomfortable. Bowing is uncomfortable.

The word humility is related to the word *humor*, and we see this hunger to escape this humiliation of humility in our humor. It's the put-down joke, the Don Rickles line of pride. Two masters of prideful humor and cutting remarks were playwright

George Bernard Shaw and politician Winston Churchill. Once, Shaw was invited to tea by a woman who was one of those nuisances who like to collect celebrities and drop their names. In typically English upper-class fashion, she invited him simply by sending him her card that read: "Lady So-and-So will be at home Thursday between 4:00 and 6:00." Shaw returned the card with this notation: "Mr. George Bernard Shaw, likewise."

Then there's the famous exchange between Churchill and stuffy Lady Astor who said, "Mr. Churchill, if I was your wife I'd poison your tea." Churchill replied: "Madam, if I was your husband, I'd drink it."

They were masters, Shaw and Churchill, of the fine art of insult. So, imagine the time they got into it with each other. Shaw sent two tickets to his new play to Churchill with this note: "These are two tickets for opening night of my new play, one for you and one for a friend, if you have one." Churchill sent the tickets back with the note: "I cannot attend opening night. Send two tickets for the next night, if there is one."

Now compare that ambition and pride to the gestures of Jesus in his last days. When we look at Jesus in Holy Week he is bowing and kneeling. But also, listen to Jesus. At his trial Jesus was silent — he never argued or put down anyone. Earlier that week when the disciples scolded him for wasting expensive ointment, when Judas offered the betrayer's kiss in the Garden of Gethsemane and swords flashed, when Caiaphas indignantly shouted, "Are you the Son of God?", Christ's reply was always calm and quiet. He never paraded himself. He never put down his accusers. He had enough self-esteem — God-given esteem — that he could absorb these attacks without being defensive. Christ knew that great secret — people can only be filled with the Holy Spirit when they first empty themselves of themselves.

Hear again Paul's words about Jesus in the letter to the Philippians: "Let the same mind be in you that was in Christ Jesus, who, though he was in the form of God, did not regard equality with God as something to be exploited, but emptied himself, taking the form of a slave..." (Philippians 2:5-7) Paul wrote this because the church in Philippi was having a church fight. People were putting down each other, insulting each other, boasting that they were better than others. No one knew how to bow. Paul's answer to the petty fights was to hold up to them the greatest act in history, as if to say, Christ humbled himself to save the world; why can't you humble yourself to end an argument? Christ humbled himself to become a slave; can't you humble yourself to become a brother or sister? Christ became obedient unto death that you might live. Won't you sacrifice your pride to say the word that brings new life to the person dying on the inside? Can't you bow?

We bow in little ways in worship. Many Christians kneel when taking communion or in the pews during confession. We instinctively bow heads when praying. We smile, shake hands, and even bow down to hug others during the passing of the peace. Such rituals help drain us of the illusion that each of us is the center of the world. A kneeling spirit is no longer full of itself. It is emptied out and thus opened for the filling of God's Spirit. When Paul urged the Philippians to be of the same mind as Christ, to imitate him in humility and obedience, he was saying, "Kneel down and empty out." Jesus emptied himself of his divinity in order to come to us in humble, human form. Shouldn't we empty ourselves of our pride in order to be filled with the divine love that Christ offered?

The words humility, humiliation, and humor all come from the same word — *humus* — the Latin word that means the earth from which we are made. Quiet Christ riding into Jerusalem on a donkey reminds all of us to be earthbound in our pride and vanity. Bow your head. Be like Jesus. As he said, "Whoever exalts himself will be humbled, and he who humbles himself will be exalted."

The exalted will be humbled. Remember the three grand buildings our ancestors built for Kaiser Wilhelm's proud processional parade? The two Lutheran churches today are still churches and are now beloved for they run relief programs for the poor, a botanical garden, and schools teaching Palestinians about their heritage. One church even started a college. And the Augusta Victoria Palace is now a hospital, the only modern hospital serving Jerusalem's Palestinians. The exalted buildings are beloved for they are willing to be humbled, to be one with the earth and its people.

The exalted will be humbled, and the humble will be exalted. Bowing does not mean being a doormat. Remember Dr. Krister Stendahl, the beloved professor with his head always lowered? Over the years publishers were eager to publish his works. Many nations and churches bestowed humanitarian awards on him. And Stendahl with his bowed head became Bishop of Stockholm, leader of the five-million-member Lutheran Church of Sweden. Perhaps even the Lord laughs at humility's humor.

Amen.

Maundy Thursday

"I want everyone to bear witness, I am the greatest! I'm the greatest thing that ever lived. I don't have a mark on my face, and I upset Sonny Liston, and I just turned 22 years old. I must be the greatest. I showed the world. I shook up the world; I'm the king of the world. You must listen to me. I am the greatest! I can't be beat!"

You know who said that (*show Muhammad Ali's picture*) — Muhammad Ali. The year was 1964 and the Louisville, Kentucky, native had just become the heavyweight champion of the world.

But now who said this — "Wouldn't it be a beautiful world if just 10% of the people who believe in the power of love would compete with one another to see who could do the most good for the most people? So many of us enjoy taking part in competitions, why not hold a competition of love instead of one that leads to jealousy and envy?" Wouldn't that be great? That's also Ali, written in his autobiography forty years later. (Mohamed Ali, *The Soul Of A Butterfly: Reflections On Life's Journey* (Simon & Schuster, New York) 2004, page XXIII)

We might explain the difference by something else Ali said: "The man who views the world at fifty the same as he did at twenty has just wasted the last thirty years of his life" (*1974 News Conference in London.*) Afflicted by Parkinson's disease for the last 32 years of his life — a condition likely brought on by the pummeling his body received in the ring — Ali spent decades as a global goodwill ambassador, peace activist, and advocate for the developing world. By one estimate, he provided over 100 million meals to feed the hungry. He hand-delivered many of those meals himself in third world countries. He remained one of the most easily recognized celebrities on the planet but for forty years did most of his charitable work quietly.

I don't know about you, but I never liked The Louisville Lip and never thought he became great until he began to serve. In his last decades, barely able to whisper, he sounded profound. When he died, they literally closed all downtown streets in Louisville for his funeral.

Jesus often talked about greatness. When James and John asked for seats of power in heaven, one on his left and one on his right, Jesus said whoever would be great must be a servant. He took children in his arms and told the disciples to become as weak, innocent, and trusting as they. At the Last Supper he told them the greatest must be as the youngest, the leader as one who serves.

You can hardly blame the disciples for wanting to be with Jesus. He was a miracle-worker. They could sense his power even when he was not doing anything extraordinary — he had this sense of gravity about him, this electricity. And if their juggling to be great seemed like gross ambition it was also profound faith. These men absolutely believed Jesus would reign.

At the Last Supper, the disciples still believed that the new world would be set up just like the old world only with new leadership in place. The bad guys at the head table would be removed, and their chairs fumigated. God's new crew would be seated, with Jesus in the number one position and the most loyal disciples on either side. Once this change had been accomplished, then — finally! At last — the good people would commence to redeem the world from top to bottom, beginning from the top. The ultimate trickle-down effect.

"It doesn't work that way," Jesus told them again. The kingdom of God is not remotely like the old kingdoms of the world. The number ones are not the powerful ones having their picture taken at the head of the table; they are the quiet ones slipping in and out among the guests, refilling wine glasses, washing feet. We've heard this so often before it is all but lost on us. The end of the line is the best place to be. The lowliest job is the one to covet. Those who serve are luckier than those in power and lovers of God get less status, not more.

It must be a test, think the disciples, like boot camp or parole — some type of intermediate step. Do your time as a servant and win a good seat in the kingdom to come. Washing the feet of a guest at dinner was the job of a slave or humblest servant in the ancient world. Not even a disciple was expected to do that. Certainly not the master should wash feet.

"It doesn't work that way," Jesus told them one more time. He was not pretending to be a servant until the time came for him to whip off his disguise and climb onto his throne; he was a servant through and through. He was not in it for reward. He was in it for the love of God, which promised him nothing but the opportunity to give himself away. The best seat he would get this side of the grave had only a wooden backrest full of splinters, and when he was hung out to dry on it by the powers that be, it wold not be James and John on either side of him but two unnamed bandits, one on his left and one on his right.

They told a legend about Saint Francis of Assisi. As a youth he was wealthy, an aristocratic, used to having others wait on him. But he felt an emptiness inside and longed for inner peace. One day as he was riding alone outside his city he saw a leper, a mass of sores, pus, and contamination that all people scorn. Normally, the fastidious Francis would be repulsed by this horrible sight of human wreckage. But something stirred within Francis. He dismounted and embraced the stunned leper. And in that embrace the leper turned into the figure of Jesus. The nearer we are to human suffering, the nearer we are to God.

If we don't understand it, let's not be too hard on ourselves. Most of our life is spent as a Maundy Thursday. Most of our life is spent focused on what we will eat and where we will sit, and can you ever find decent help with that foot washing? When we glimpse Jesus most days, he is still serving us, still feeding us, still giving himself away.

But someday the climax of our life will come, and like the centurion we will look up at the broken figure on the cross whispering compassionate words and we'll say, "Surely this was the Son of God." That's when we realize that serving is how we transform the world, not from the top down but from the bottom up. It a trickle-up effect. You're not the champion of the world until you look down from whatever cross you're on, can barely whisper, and still find ways to serve. A competition to serve.

Amen.

The Unseen Cross
Beside Him

Some time ago I went out to lunch with a friend who is a Baptist minister. Scott is a bright, compassionate man and the differences in our background make for good conversation. At one point he leaned over the table and said, "You Lutherans are about to enter Lent. What in the world is Lent?"

I tried to explain the forty days of reflection on Jesus' passion, this six-week period that climaxes on Good Friday. He listened closely and then reflected, "So Lent is really the time you keep the cross always before you."

Right. But that insight is not as easy as you think. Few of us really want a cross on our shoulder. At that famous scene when Jesus asked Peter "Who am I?" and Peter hemmed and hawed and finally said, "You are the Christ," we usually celebrate the insight and faith. We forget the next words of the gospel, "And then Jesus began to teach them that the Son of Man must suffer... and be rejected... and be killed." We forget that Peter had a fit at those words and Jesus had to admonish him, "Get behind me, Satan." Jesus' words struck at the heart of our expectation for deliverance — Jesus' words *suffer, rejected, killed.*

When I served a downtown church, it was customary for pastors to exchange pulpits and do sermon series. One year on Good Friday a dozen clergy gathered at the biggest church for a three-hour worship marathon — noon to three — with seven of us each preaching on one of the seven last words on the cross. People would come and go throughout the three hours, but one thing remained constant — no preacher wanted to talk about the cross. Everyone bypassed Lent, suffering, the

Passion, the trial, and crucifixion. One preacher mentioned the cross but only as a springboard to the resurrection. "We know Jesus died on the cross, but it was only a temporary setback on the road to the empty tomb." There were seven Easter sermons that year before the sun had even gone down on Good Friday.

No one wants a cross — not for Jesus, not for us. To avoid it our theologies minimize our involvement in evil and inflate our potential for good. Sin is explained away as a setback for society that can be overcome through sincere effort. Evil is a maladjustment that can be fixed through sociological or psychological tinkering. Unable to be obedient or courageous we are content to be decent. Our shoulders are not comfortable with the load of a cross.

Bonhoeffer said of carrying a cross, "Pain is a holy angel who shows us treasures that would otherwise remain forever hidden; through him men and women have become greater than through all the joys of the world." But such pain we avoid. Before a cross we cringe.

And yet, I think God silently screams at us on Good Friday, "Remember the cross." I'm not superstitious but I'm convinced every Good Friday when I was a child the weather was dark and threatening. Thunderstorms howled. "Don't run from the cross," God whistled in the wind.

They tell me in the southeast the pine trees know when it's Good Friday. If you look at the tops of the pine trees a week or two before Easter, you'll notice the yellow shoots. As the days draw near to Good Friday the shoots branch off and form a cross. By this day the tops of the pines are filled with yellow crosses.

They tell me throughout the south the Dogwood blossoms know when it's Good Friday. The dogwood blooms for a very short time near the date of the crucifixion. The flower has just four petals representing the hands and feet of Christ. Each petal would be marked with a hole at the edge and shaded with red, the blood of Christ. The center of the flower would be circular, raised, and representing the head of Christ wearing the crown of thorns.

Or look at the animal on which Jesus rode into Jerusalem. Seen from above, every donkey has a dark cross on its back from shoulder blade to shoulder blade, and from neck to tail. Jesus entered Jerusalem on a cross and left it on a cross.

"Remember the cross." It's not just nature. Drive down the street. Every telephone pole is a dark cross. Every window in an old house has four panes of glass separated by a wooden cross.

This is the season when the cross is always on our mind. Not just seeing the cross — but living it. Jesus said, "Take up your cross and follow me." There are unseen crosses everywhere. Whenever we sacrifice for another there is a cross. Whenever we take on a burden we could have ignored because taking it on is the right thing to do there is a cross. Whenever a young peacekeeper soldier is killed in a bombing overseas because he is focused on serving his country, there is a cross.

Suffering alone does not make an unseen cross. Anyone can suffer in our fallen world. Taking up a cross is agreeing to endure the suffering because you think it is the right thing to do. You accept the suffering because some service is performed, some dignity is respected, some harmony with the Father is found.

There was a time when the Lutheran clergy in the city I once served were generally young, eager, and close. We celebrated when someone got married, someone had a baby, someone accepted a new call. Early one fall we were laughing because one shy young pastor and his wife announced they were having a baby. Then, in winter came the whispers — something was wrong. The baby wasn't developing right. The whispers — they should do something while they still could, they should not have to suffer. Finally, as spring arrived the quiet pastor said the words — we know the baby cannot live, we know the baby must be born. And so it was — a birth, a baptism, a baby held for an hour and then she was gone. No one asked the mother and father their reasons. Everyone offered their response with a word, a touch, or a tear.

For months we noticed a look in their eyes, as if they had been given a burden not too heavy for them at all, as if it were light, a privilege, borne on another's shoulders, being led to a high place the rest of us could not go, following a sign the rest of us did not see. *(project the shadow of a cross on screen)*

Amen.

Easter Sunday

John 20:1-18 or Matthew 28:1-10

Afraid? Not Here

(Note — for a longer, richer sermon, replace paragraphs 5 and 6 with the addendum at the end of this sermon.)

Are you facing a crisis? Perhaps an illness, financial ruin, or family breakup. Certainly, the nation has faced many crises this decade. The Afghanistan debacle, wars in Ukraine and Israel and looming war in Asia, political corruption in Washington, recession, broken borders leading to thirteen million illegal migrants in the US. We always seem to be in a crisis.

In the darkness of Easter morning the disciples — men and women — were in crisis. Their dreams had died on the cross of Christ. They knew that soon the government would hunt down and kill Jesus' friends. How would they cope with their crisis? How do you handle a crisis?

The truth is every great event in the Bible begins as a crisis. Abraham is homeless when God promises a homeland, the promised land. Jacob is sold by his brothers into slavery in Egypt; if he had not been there, he could not have saved his family from a famine with Egyptian food. The Exodus was an escape from slavery. No giant Goliath, no David and his slingshot. Seventy years after the Babylonians destroyed Jerusalem and carried the Judeans off into captivity they returned with three new features — a book we call the Old Testament, a name — Jews — and a new backbone. And what about the unwed pregnant teenager on a donkey with her fiancée looking for a room in Bethlehem? Each a crisis.

Perhaps the greatest crisis of this century to date is Covid-19. Seven million people died worldwide; more than a million died in the US. How do you overcome a world-wide crisis?

Look at the closest parallel to Covid-19. Think of the greatest pandemic in history. It's been called the greatest disaster in human history — the Plague, the Black Death of the middle of the fourteenth century. The Plague started in central Asia in 1347, carried by fleas on the backs of rats. By 1350 the Black Death was in all of Europe. Within four years the Plague killed one-third of the people of Europe and before it ended Europe lost half of its population. It made people question their faith in a God many felt had abandoned them. It destroyed their confidence in medieval medicine. It destroyed the feudal structure of society, forcing many serfs off their overlord's land where serfs had lived for generations. It was epic disaster!

But something else happened because of the Plague. Europe was no longer overpopulated and underfed. There was more food for the survivors which led to better health. Medieval medical myths were abandoned in favor of observation and experimentation, what we call modern science, as hospitals became places for healing, not merely dying. Medieval religious customs were questioned which led to the Protestant Reformation. The end of serfdom didn't only force people off their landlords' estates, it allowed people to be independent. The workday grew longer and people worked more, were more driven. They were working for themselves now, not for the local nobility, which led to personal ambition, which led to the rise of the middle class and of cities. The Plague ended the stoic Medieval resignation to the pain and suffering of your place in life and a rise of proactive ambition — people wanted a more active life, to "Get ahead in life." It was the beginning of humanism. It was the beginning of the Renaissance, the beginning of the modern world. Ask historians for a rough date for the beginning of the Renaissance and they will say 1350 — the same date as the Bubonic Plague! From Plague crisis came blossoming culture!

This brings us back to the gospel and the Easter story. We often are in a crisis today. That's what the disciples felt that

Holy Week, also — they're in a crisis. The disciples on Easter morning were holed-up in their rented homes. They were confused and afraid. They were not all together. It sounds like us today. When the women arrived at the tomb Easter morning they had a Black Death mood — grief, depression, a resignation that life was nothing more than disappointment and suffering and loss. Then they saw the tomb was empty. They assumed it was another disaster, that someone had stolen the Lord's body. But at that empty tomb they also met an angel.

Six times in the gospel are stories of angels appearing to people. In four of those six times the first thing the angel said was, "Do not fear." The other times the angel said first, "Why are you weeping?" or, "Why do you seek the living among the dead?" In Matthew's gospel, the first words of Jesus to the women on Easter are, "Greetings. Fear not." Don't be afraid!

I am not minimalizing our current concern and caution during war, corruption, or pandemic. But God's promise is for new life. God works in surprising ways. Who could have imagined the most shameful, painful means of death — a crucifixion -- God would use to show God's love for the world and God's power over death in the resurrection? Who could have imagined that a pandemic would bring America's partisan politicians together, or prompt selfless sacrifice by health-care workers?

Who could have imagined the first thing the resurrected Lord said to Mary on Easter morning was the same thing we germ-fearing older adults said to our children and grandchildren in those pandemic times — "Do not touch me — It's not the time for that yet."

One message of Easter is that God is unpredictable. Saint Paul in Romans 8:28 wrote, "In the same way, the Spirit helps us in our weakness. We do not know what we ought to pray for, but the Spirit himself intercedes for us through wordless groans." Crisis prompts the wordless groans; God's surprise prompts our inability to pray as we ought, for we can't imagine the surprises God has in store.

In a crisis, the routines you depend on disappear. God sends you to live in a new city or gives you a new challenge at work or allows a pandemic to strike and it takes you from your secure little world, forcing us to grow in faith and in creativity and dependence on God. It's unnerving to follow God because we like life to be tidy, we like to have all the answers — we can't fathom American businesses all shut down or tent hospitals in Central Park of New York. We can't image God on a cross or how a grave can be empty. But God often uses crises that we can't understand until later. As Isaiah says to God, "Your ways are higher than my ways and your thoughts higher than my thoughts." Perhaps it's inevitable that like the women at the tomb we are unnerved and afraid unless we have all the answers. "Afraid — he's not here" is what they felt and thought.

That's why it's important to hear the angel's message. For at the empty tomb the angels do not say, "Happy Easter" or "Be of good cheer." They say, "Why are you weeping?" and "Be not afraid." Be not afraid — for the one who is risen is the Christ we've learned to trust. Be not afraid for Christ will be with us if we call on him and with the recognition of him the fear and the grief disappear, leaving room for joy. "Then the disciples were glad when they saw the Lord," says the Gospel. So, Easter put flesh in John's words: "There is no fear in love, for perfect love casts out fear."

You know the old saying by Plato, "Necessity is the mother of invention." Today we can say crisis is the mother of innovation and innovation inspires.

Crises don't last forever. Ingenuity, goodwill, forgiveness, courage, and common sense can crush a crisis. In 1861, the United States was famous for slavery and racism. After a gruesome Civil War and 160 years of Civil Rights struggles, today the US is the most integrated large nation in the world. The Census Bureau says there is a 61% chance that any two Americans chosen at random will be of different races or ethnicities. Racism is abhorred.

Over ten weeks in late 1929, the stock market crashed, and the businesses of America lost half of their value to begin the Great Depression. Twenty years later this nation and its citizens were stronger and wealthier than ever and programs such as Unemployment Compensation and Social Security added a national sense of security.

In the Spring of 1945, Europe was bitterly divided by war and the two most evil governments in the world were Hitler's Germany and Tojo's Japan. Five years later, Japan and Germany had two of the most democratic governments, the world was at peace, the UN had been formed, and NATO united most of Europe. Eighty years later NATO has doubled in size and the UN has tripled.

And it is not only nations that overcome crises. The trauma can be personal. Before he knew Christ, Saul was as righteous and accomplished as a religious person could be. He was cocky and cocksure. "If any other person thinks he has reason for self-confidence, I can assure him I have more," he said of himself (Philippians 3:4). Then came his conversion experience crisis where God knocked him to the ground, blinded him, gave him a "thorn in the flesh," prompted his friends to condemn him as evil, and left him in the care of former enemies in a hostile city. He later escaped being killed in that city by being lowered in a basket over the city wall at night. How could life get any worse? But in that crisis God tenderized the heart of Saul, deepened his soul, and sharpened his mind to confess he had been lost but now was found by Christ's love. And from his crisis his name was transformed — Saul was gone, Saint Paul was born.

The trauma of crisis can be personal. Nelson Mandela was a quiet South African Methodist goaded by the injustice of apartheid to become a revolutionary. But then came 27 years in prison and tuberculosis and failing eyesight. His later friend, Bishop Desmond Tutu, said Mandela went into prison "one of the most angry of men.... But the suffering of those 27 years helped to purify him and grow the magnanimity that would become his hallmark." Jail helped Mandela learn how to turn enemies into friends. It also gave him an unassailable credibility that allowed him to be his nation's first black president. "When you speak of forgiveness, 27 years in prison sets you up very nicely," said Tutu.

The trauma of crisis can be personal. Frank Siller was a Staten Island, New York, financial advisor when the disaster hit. It was 9/11 and his brother, Steven Siller, was a fireman killed in the twin towers collapse. Frank was inspired to start Tunnel to Towers, a charity with an A+ rating that has raised more than a half billion dollars to house more than 400 families of fallen first responders or displaced former service personnel.

The trauma of crisis can be personal and not only for famous people. Jon White was a captain in the British Royal Marines serving in Afghanistan. In 2010, an explosion ripped off his legs beneath the knees and his right arm below the elbow. He went back to England and to his fiancée, Becky, with a medical discharge and pension. Now he needed a job and a home that could accommodate him. His only skill set was leading and organizing men and their loyalty to him. So, he prayed. Soon builders and skilled tradesmen offered to mentor him and his fiancée to build their own house. Former comrades from the Marines — some also disabled — came to lend a hand. White served as project manager. The experience helped him cope with his trauma. The British TV program *Grand Designs* profiled the story of his new home. Jon and Becky are now married with a child. Jon's new career is mentoring disabled people building homes as well as giving motivational talks. Becky says the years since his injury have been the happiest, most fulfilling years of their lives.

Crises don't last forever. People filled with God's Spirit can overcome a crisis. The Chinese phrase we translate as the word crisis is a combination of two words — danger and opportunity. Let's use each crisis as an opportunity for new medicines, new volunteer cooperation for the public good, new harmony, new government reform, an opportunity for a new Renaissance. An opportunity for new faith.

God's "yes" will simply not tolerate our "no's", or life's "no's" or death's "no's." Easter is about entering the mystery of God with confidence. For those who in pain, bewilderment, loneliness, or fear lift up their tentative faces in hope of seeing his face, this elusive face of God gazes back in love. Afraid? Not here!

Amen.

Addendum

Look at the closest parallel to Covid-19. Think of the greatest pandemic in history. It's been called the greatest disaster in human history — the Plague, the Black Death of the middle of the fourteenth century. The Plague started in central Asia in 1347, carried by fleas on the backs of rats. By 1350 the Black Death was in all of Europe. The first major city hit was Constantinople; half of the city died. Many people fled west carrying the disease with them, with many landing in Italy.

One-third of Florence died in six months; half of Milan and Venice in eighteen months; half of the region of Tuscany. The pope had twelve physicians — five died.

Spreading north, one-third of Paris died (500 people a day died at its height)

20% of Germany;

40% of England;

45% of Scandinavia

60% of Iceland

All Viking settlements in Greenland were abandoned.

Between 1347 and 1353 a third of Europe died!

The Plague subsided by 1350 but then it returned every five to fifteen years in smaller waves and kept returning for the next sixty years. By the early 1400's the population of Europe was only 50% or 60% of what it had been in 1290, a loss of nearly half the population in 130 years!

This crisis led to grief, fear, depression, a breakdown of community feeling. People had emotional social distancing, afraid even of their spouses and children. Many towns simply disappeared. There was a sense of guilt. People thought that God was punishing them, that people must have sinned to deserve this.

Religion was undermined in people's minds for churches and mosques did not provide adequate solace, support, or explanation. In 1350, people felt abandoned by God, much as the disciples did in the dark, early hours of Easter morning.

But something else came from the Bubonic Plague crisis. People changed. People discovered new life. The Plague spurred the rise of modern medicine based on observation and testing and not old wives' tales. Communities created hospitals as places to heal and not simply to isolate the ill. They improved public sanitation.

Before the plague farms had been overworked and could not produce enough food so people were malnourished. After the plague a smaller population meant more food for the survivors so now most people had enough to eat which increased health and productivity; in many places the average person's daily calorie intake went from 1100 calories to 1900 calories.

The loss of population meant the end of serfdom; in the Middle Ages ¾ of people in Europe and Russia had been serfs. These were not slaves, but they were not free to leave the farms of their birth. After the Plague people in Europe were not compelled to work the land where they were born as a virtual slave of their lord — they were free to find their own occupation. In the Middle Ages serfs labored five to six hours a day, just enough to put food on the table and clothes on the back. After the challenge of the Plague the workday grew longer and people worked more, were more driven. They were working for themselves now which led to personal ambition.

Land that was poor cropland such as in Spain was allowed to become pastureland — more sheep and cattle — more protein and better health. With fewer people in Europe workers were in more demand which led to a rise in wages.

Surviving the plague and finding more freedom meant the end of stoic Medieval resignation to the pain and suffering of your place in life and a rise of proactive ambition — people wanted a more active life, to "Get ahead in life." It also meant freedom to travel. Before the plague most Europeans never travelled more than twenty miles from where they were born.

With old stereotypes broken and health improving people began to explore. They explored the world, sailing around Africa to the Far East, sailing west to the New World. They also explored inventions. Necessity was the mother of invention and so clocks were invented to help people schedule their busier workday. Rifles were invented and harpsichords, pumps and cogwheels for mining, double-entry bookkeeping, the first translation of the Bible into English, and ninety years later, the printing press (the most important of all inventions).

Because Constantinople in Greece was the first city struck with the plague, scores of Greek scholars escaped, fleeing to northern Italy, the most advanced place in Europe in 1350. These men brought with them the works of Plato, Aristotle, and the classical Greek historians and playwrights. The Italians loved this art and literature, and they jump-started Europe's love affair with the classical world. Will Durant called it "the energizing yeast in the rising body of European thought."

The Greek classics gave rise to Humanism with its emphasis, "Man is the measure of all things" — that people are the center of the universe. With Humanism came a rise in self-confidence and personal drive. Humanism also meant people were not constrained by old church teachings and the people now challenging those old dogmas would soon give rise to the Protestant Reformation. It also led to new inventions. Inventions in century that followed 1350 — guns, eyeglasses, scales for weights, oil paints, golf balls, public library, coil springs. In breaking the old world of medieval feudalism, the plague freed people to invent a new Europe.

People being freer and working harder meant a rise in per capita productivity. Europe became prosperous. Prosperity meant better diets, better mental health, and better general health. Soon came the creation of the middle class.

It was the birth of the Renaissance! Ask historians when did the Medieval World end and the Renaissance begin — they will say about the same time the Black Death struck, about the year 1350. From Plague crisis came blossoming culture.

No Doubt

(Images of the famous people mentioned here and of Golf's The Human Chain can be found online.)

If I mention Saint Thomas from the Bible, how do you refer to him? Probably his nickname, "Doubting Thomas." Poor man — One slip-up questioning the resurrection and he's branded for eternity. But have we misnamed Saint Thomas? The world knows the man in this Sunday's scripture as Doubting Thomas. But is doubting so bad? Frederick Buechner writes, "Doubts are the ants in the pants of faith — they keep it alive and moving." (Frederick Buechner, *Wishful Thinking: A Theological ABC* (Harper & Row, New York) 1973 pp. 25-26) In Genesis in the Old Testament a stranger appears to Jacob one evening and says he is an angel from God. Right! Jacob wrestles with the stranger all night and at dawn the angel says, "You get a new name. No longer are you Jacob; you are now Israel" (which means, "wrestles with God"). In Exodus a burning bush speaks to Moses who asks, "Who are you?" The bush replies, "I am God." Right! But Moses obeys God's voice and returns to Egypt to lead the Exodus. God's people have long questioned the Almighty to better understand and believe. Doubting's not dumb.

Perhaps we should call Saint Thomas *Daring Thomas*. A few weeks before Easter, Jesus said he was going to Jerusalem where his life was in danger. The other disciples say that's crazy and urge him not to go. It was Thomas who said, "Let us also go, that we might die with him." Thomas was willing to die. He was daring!

Perhaps a better nickname would be *Disillusioned Thomas*. This disciple thought Jesus had let him down. He wanted in religion what so many people want — a grand display of power and pomp. He wanted to end his worries about the decay of his nation and the threat to the disciples by King Herod and his goons. From where Thomas stood Jesus' story ended not in triumph but in a tomb. He didn't realize that suffering and death were part of God's plan.

Certainly, he could be called *Discouraged Thomas*. Ask one-hit wonders why no great sequel and they will usually say they surrendered to discouragement in their subsequent work. But obstacles — are opportunities — to overcome — opposition. I know of a lawyer who was so discouraged and depressed that his friends quietly put away all razors and knives out of his sight. During his darkness he wrote: "I am now the most miserable man living.... Whether I shall ever be better I cannot tell. I have a foreboding I will not. To remain as I am is impossible; I must die or be better." And he did get better. He persevered and nineteen years later this lawyer, Abraham Lincoln, was elected president.

One name we cannot give Thomas is *Deserting Thomas*. Notice where Thomas is in this gospel reading. He is in the upper room, back in the fellowship, back with the disciples. He could have made excuses and wrapped himself in gloom and stayed at home. We see that all the time. People go through a difficult time and the first thing they say is, "God abandoned me. Church isn't worth it." They miss one Sunday, then a second, and before long it takes more effort to go to worship with friends than to make excuses for staying home. But Thomas knew something about this fellowship of disciples. He knew it was the place where people cared for him. It was this caring, not a confidence in an empty tomb, that brought him back the week after Easter. Thomas trusted his friends.

Faith is more about trusting some*one* than knowing some*thing*. Faith is more than believing ideas; it is believing *in* someone. This man has become *Determined Thomas*!

In 1987, The Bing Crosby Pro-Am Golf Tournament was played in Monterey, California, overlooking the ocean. The tournament had the actors Jack Lemmon and Clint Eastwood paired with golfers Peter Jacobson and Greg Norman. On the sixteenth hole, Jack Lemmon's ball rolled several yards down the side of a cliff and landed on a plant. Lemmon wanted to take a bogey, but Eastwood encouraged him to take the shot. He promised to hold on to his friend's belt to keep him from falling the seventy feet into the ocean. Jack Lemmon trusted Clint Eastwood. He agreed to try the shot. He was determined. Jacobson then grabbed Eastwood's arm to keep them both safe and Norman held the back of Jacobson's belt to save them all. Lemmon's semi-miraculous shot made the green and the whole affair became golf legend as "The Human Chain." (Forget the fact that Lemmon's next shot sent the ball into the sea.)

Now that's trust. How many people do you know that you would trust to hold you over a seventy-feet cliff? The church term for such trust is "faith."

Maybe we should also call this saint *Dreaming Thomas*. It was Thomas during the Last Supper who asked Jesus the way where he was going and Jesus replied with those most evocative words, "I AM the way, and the truth, and the life; no one comes to the Father, but by me." Jesus was stretching Thomas' vison, his imagination. "Why couldn't you imagine I was resurrected?" Jesus was saying. In a sense, Jesus was calling on Thomas to pretend. Pretend! That word, pretend, originally did not mean a fanciful idea. It is from the Latin word meaning "to put forward" to see something before it arrived. Stretch your imagination.

True story — My father had a small plumbing company, and the office manager was named Herman. Herman and his wife, Esther, were Mennonites. Mennonites were like the Amish, only not so austere. The Amish don't drive cars; Mennonites seemed to drive only old, plain Chevrolets. Amish don't have televisions or telephones; Mennonites had radios and black landline phones with dials. These were wonderful, salt-of-the-earth people. When I was a shy teenage boy my mother and Esther set me up on a blind date with Herman's and Esther's daughter, Rosemary. It was for her senior prom. Now, Rosemary was attractive and gracious, but she was also deaf in one ear and hard of hearing in the other. "How can this evening work if we can barely communicate?" I ask. My mother replies — "Pretend. If you pretend that you're having a good time you'll probably end up having a good time, and then it's not pretending anymore." And that's what happens. At dinner in the gym in her country high school, beneath papier mâché ornaments with an Arabian Nights theme, I sit on her side that has an ear of some faint hearing, and I tap her foot when I speak so she would look at me. She reads lips and laughs as if I really was clever. When she speaks in the sometimes hard to understand speech of the deaf, I nod and smile as if I understand. And sometimes I did understand, at least I understand her eagerness to fit in with her classmates and earn their admiring eye. We two pretend to have a good time and in the pretending, we bond in our secret and do have a good time. We stretch our imagination. For that evening, Rosemary is an Arabian Nights princess who does belong. Abraham Lincoln put it so well once: "People are about as happy as they make up their minds to be."

When Jesus met the disciples in the upper room the week after Easter, most of the disciples did not have to pretend to believe in the resurrection. On Easter night they had seen Jesus in the flesh, or what surely looked like flesh, so they knew, they *knew*. But Thomas had not been there. He could not know for sure, he said. So now on this night a week later when Jesus appeared he gently scolds Thomas for his lack of faith. Jesus tells him, "Blessed are those who have not seen and yet have come to believe." Christ is describing how faith for us begins. Not with certainty, but with trust, with wanting. If you pretend Christ will be with you invisibly, then in time you'll sense he is with you, and it's not pretending anymore.

Faith begins with make-believe. Saint Augustine said it eloquently. After saying his heart was on fire for the Lord, Augustine said, "Faith is to believe what you do not yet see, and the reward for this faith is to see what you believe." Believe that you might see. Have faith, even if it seems like pretending, and what you pretend will become real, will become clear. Frederick Buechner writes for Thomas as well as for us: "Faith is not being sure where you are going but going anyway. A journey without maps..." What do they say about beauty, that it's in the eye of the beholder? The same with faith. It doesn't come because you've proven something or other about God. You see Christ, trust Christ, because you long to.

Buechner adds: "Almost nothing that makes any real difference can be proved. I can prove the law of gravity by dropping a shoe out of the window. I can prove the earth is round if I'm clever at that sort of thing — that the radio works, that light travels faster than sound. I cannot prove that life is better than death or love better than hate. I cannot prove the greatness of the great or the beauty of the beautiful. I cannot prove my own free will... Faith can't prove a damned thing. Or a blessed thing either."

Faith begins with make-believe. You become what you pretend to be.

Little Anjeze Bojaxhiu of North Macedonia grew up pretending to heal injured neighborhood pets. Today she is remembered as the angel of Calcutta, Mother Teresa.

Elias was a shy, insecure Missouri boy who spent his mornings helping his impoverished father deliver newspapers. To escape the boredom Elias began to sketch, losing himself in his cartoons. He was good at dreaming and drawing, and in time, with the help of his little friend, Mickey Mouse, Walt Elias Disney earned 26 Academy Awards and began what today is the largest film studio in Hollywood.

Young Archibald Leach escaped dysfunctional parents and poverty in England by becoming an actor. He invented a new persona, developed a totally fake, unique accent, and took the stage name Cary Grant.

Karol Józef Wojtyła was also an actor. He lived in Poland as a teenager before leaving acting to become a priest serving the poorest district of Krakow. He pretended he could defeat Communism with simple courage and Christ's love. Then pretend becomes truth. The Soviet Union fell and Father Karol becomes Pope John Paul II.

As for Saint Thomas, imagination took him farther than anyone. Tradition says Thomas took the faith to India twenty years after the resurrection. But no one in Israel heard from him again. In 1498, when European explorers rounded the Cape of Good Hope on the southern edge of Africa and first landed in southern India, they were amazed to find a long-established Christian presence. There were thousands of Christians. And scores of their churches were named Saint Thomas. Of that, there is no doubt.

Oh, yes — my blind date, Rosemary. The last I saw of her was several years after that high school prom. She was on the back of a blessedly deafening Harley motorcycle, holding on to her new husband, heading off to college, her face ablaze with joy. She had become the princess she once had only pretended to be.

Amen.

Where You Least Expect

Kate Winslet and Jack Black are two of the stars in the Christmas romance movie *The Holiday*. In one scene they are in a Los Angeles DVD store looking at movies to buy. Black's character picks up a copy of *The Graduate*. He doesn't notice that standing a few feet behind him is Dustin Hoffman. Hoffman shakes his head and mutters, "Can't go anywhere." Turns out Hoffman, who had starred in *The Graduate* nearly forty years earlier, on the morning of that filming of *The Holiday* had been driving down the LA street, saw the camera crew and recognized the movie's director. He had pulled over to say hello. The director quietly asked him to make the quick cameo. He's in and out so fast most people on set don't realize he's there.

That sounds a little like Mary on Easter morning. She's gazing at the empty tomb when the gardener walks up. She asks the man where they had taken Jesus. Not until he speaks does Mary realize the man beside her is Jesus. Likewise, ten or twelve hours later, on the road to Emmaus, the two disciples don't realize the stranger walking beside them is Jesus. They look at but don't really see the one walking a few feet away.

The divine is hard to pin down. If your understanding of Easter is a little fuzzy, join the crowd. Each of the gospel writers told the Easter story in a different way. One says Mary Magdalene went alone to the tomb; the other gospels say two women or three or at least four were there. Two gospels say one angel met the women; one gospel says two angels. John's gospel alone reports Mary meeting Jesus outside the tomb. These are the jumbled reports of eyewitnesses, not crafted works of fiction. No one tried to reconcile the differing accounts. They had no desire to convince us these events happened; they only eagerly report what they had experienced. The divine is hard to pin down.

Apparently the two men on the Emmaus Road heard the reports from the women about the empty tomb. They're confused. We don't know why there are going to Emmaus. Maybe in frustration they had given up on Jesus and were going home. God's ways seemed just too strange. The stranger who falls in step with them on the road explains scripture, but the two men don't quite get what he's saying. There's the irony — like Mary they are face-to-face with Jesus but in their shock and grief with the crucifixion they cannot see God working among them. That can happen to us, too, can't it? You lose hope, you discard your dreams, and you are blinded to the good things still surrounding you.

Leith Anderson is a pastor and author. He grew up outside of New York City and as a child was the most devout fan of the old Brooklyn Dodgers. One day, his father took him to a World Series game between the Dodgers and the Yankees. He was so excited for he knew his Dodgers would crush the Yankees. Unfortunately, not a single Dodger ever got on base and his excitement was shattered.

Many years later, he was talking with a man who inhaled baseball stories. Leith told him about the first major league game he attended and added, "It was such a disappointment. I was a Dodger fan and the Dodgers never got on base."

The man said, "You were there? You were there in 1956 when Don Larsen pitched the only perfect game in World Series history?"

Leith replied, "Yeah, but uh, we lost."

He then realized that he had been so demoralized by his team's defeat that he overlooked the fact that he was a witness to one of the greatest moments in sports history.

"You were there?" Have you ever caught your breath sensing you are at the center of a vortex of history. Neil Armstrong walks on the moon. The Iron Curtain falls within weeks. A hundred million people cheer in unison at the once-in-a-century solar eclipse.

Or do we get too caught up in the daily drudgery and defeats of life — the illness that lingers, the job that dulls the spirit, the financial hardship? We can be so blinded by the "defeats" that we are oblivious to the far greater works God is doing in the world and in our lives.

Saint Paul knew this. Writing from prison to the church in Philippi, Paul wrote: "My dear friends, I want you to know that what has happened to me has really served to advance the gospel." The Philippians may have puzzled at Paul's words. Why would a man in prison be grateful? Well, often when Paul was in prison he was chained to his guard. But Paul used prison as a time to talk to these soldier guards who were always beside him, to talk about Christ and to demonstrate in his own gracious behavior the love of God. Some of these soldiers were converted. Within a hundred years there was a higher percentage of Christians among the Roman army than in the general population. Two hundred fifty years later Roman General Constantine saw how strong Christianity was in his army and as he declared himself the new emperor he pointed to the cross saying, "In this sign, conquer." A kind, radiant prisoner was a seed; an empire converted was the growth.

Can we appreciate advantages in adversity? Don't let temporary disappointments blind you to the good that God is doing in your life and through your life. Jacob's teenager son, Joseph, was sold to slave traders by his jealous big brothers and ended up in an Egyptian prison; if that horror had not happened, he never would have risen to become chancellor of Egypt and able to feed his repentant brothers and their families during a famine. Don't assume that any disappointment is God's last word on any situation. God is working, if only we can see beyond our distress to the divine.

The followers of Jesus certainly had their dreams turned to dust. The last thing they expected was to discover that Christ was alive and beside them. Perhaps this is why they did not recognize him. They were blinded by their problems and couldn't see that, in Paul's words, "All things work together for good for those who love God"(Romans 8:28). When you are bent low with your problems you can't see the horizon.

One way to see Christ is to look for Christ in the people around you. My godfather, Ed Driscoll, was the pastor of my home church in the years before I was born. He and his wife, Sarah, left to serve another church in another state but came back for my baptism. As a child and teenager, I never knew Ed as the dynamic preacher and singer and evangelist that my parents loved and respected. I only remember these two people after Sarah had a stroke and for years Ed wheeled her around in her wheelchair. She was withered and could barely speak but she could always smile. I remember Ed had a booming laugh and was constantly gentle and considerate, respecting and helping his wife. He would encourage her to speak with her halting words when it would have been easier for him to carry the conversation. He would wheel her into a room before he entered. He always showed joy and love in her presence.

When I decided to be a pastor and entered seminary Ed commented that he was sorry that I never got to know him as a pastor. I can't imagine what he meant.

The highlight of today's gospel reading is the moment at supper when these little-known disciples recognize Jesus is across the table. "Were not our hearts burning within us while he talked with us on the road and opened the scriptures to us?"

The change in these disciples this evening was that at dinner they began to believe they could see Jesus. The stranger on the road who seemed strange, became the guest at the table, and then he became the host for the dinner. Funny how we still call the bread of communion "the host." Jesus meant it when he said of communion, "Where two or three are gathered together in my name, there I am with them." They began to recognize the Jesus who had always been there with them.

John Calvin once said the Bible is like a pair of eyeglasses. It's not meant to fill us with information but to sharpen our sensitivity and heighten our eagerness to spot Jesus around us. There's a reason that the only people who saw Jesus after the resurrection were his followers — people who already believed in him and were looking for him. You've heard the phrase "seeing is believing"? Well, sometimes believing is seeing — you have to trust and believe before God becomes real to you.

These two disciples had enough faith that when Jesus at the table spoke the familiar communion words, "Take, eat, this is my body....", their faith was jump-started. We continue to trust that Christ is really present in our communion even if invisible. But recognition is not limited to the familiar words of ritual of the sacrament. The familiar words of blessing may come in a conversation of hope and encouragement from a friend. Or the familiar words may come in an expression of care and concern from another, and our hope is renewed. Reminded of a time when God was familiar, rather than a stranger, we are uplifted and given hope that Christ really is alive and that God, for all God's strangeness, is faithful to the promise to be present, even to the end of time. Christ is Emmanuel — God with us.

Perhaps the stranger is recognizable to you when we are the ones who respond in love and concern and charity to the needs of other people. As the Gospel of John says, "If anyone will *do* his will, that person shall know.... "(John 7:17) I know when I am down in the dumps I may visit a person in the hospital or a shut-in and offer prayer and communion and then the God who may have been a stranger to me earlier in the day becomes recognizable in the breaking of the bread.

Isn't this how faith works? Believing is seeing. Doing is seeing.

Sometime when you visit Disneyland or Disneyworld keep your eyes open. The creators of those parks did something ingenious that you may not realize unless you look for it. They hid discreet images of Mickey Mouse throughout the park. The images are simple — three connected circles that look like the mouse's head and ears. Even the buttons in elevators on Disney property are shaped like the three circles. Many park visitors look at the circles but don't really see them. But when someone points out the circles of ears and face, then visitors see them pop up out of the woodwork, literally. They've surrounded you all day but only when you look for them do you see them.

Look through the eyes of faith and you see God's handiwork. See God's handiwork, in turn, and your faith increases and so does your awareness of God's presence all around.

Perhaps we don't see Christ before us because we're dulled by the search, like looking at the same face in the mirror for decades. Perhaps we need to hear God's voice to recognize the Lord. Some sixty years after the Emmaus Road story Saint John wrote the book of Revelation. In a passage that echoes these two disciples inviting Jesus to dinner, John wrote: "Behold, I stand at the door and knock. If anyone hears my voice and opens the door, I will come in to him and dine with him, and he with me" (Revelation 3:20).

Everett was a large, distinguished man — broad shoulders and broad smile. A retired policeman, he was courtly and kind. His wife, Fern, hair always awry, smiled constantly and spoke softly. Too softly, really, to be understood. Every other week I would meet Everett on Thursday morning in Fern's room. Each week he and I would visit and would talk with Fern, hoping that she could understand our words or at least our love. But always we met her glassy gaze and soft babble. Alzheimer had robbed her of reality. Then came one morning, more than a year after the disease had taken her from us. The communion elements spread on the coffee table, we bowed our heads to say the Lord's Prayer. "Our Father, who art in heaven," Everett's voice and mine, steady with the beloved words. "Thy kingdom come, thy will be done." Suddenly Everett gasped. There was a third voice speaking, as loud and clear as she sounded twenty years earlier. "Give us this day..." Somehow Fern had returned. Her eyes sparkled with recognition, for she was speaking the prayer to us as much as to God. "Forgive us our..." Now it was Everett's and my eyes clouding. "Deliver us from evil." By prayer's end only two voices spoke clear and loud for Everett was now sobbing. With the "Amen" the cloud descended again. But for a few moments the Holy Spirit was present where we least expected the Spirit.

Today's gospel reading ends abruptly: "And he vanished out of their sight." Which is to say you cannot nail God down to a dining room table and the breaking of bread any more than you can keep God on a cross with real nails. The two Emmaus travelers wanted him to stay. They wanted to rehash the marvelous experience. But God would not be part of deadly-dull postmortems. "He vanished out of their sight."

It would be wonderful to always be able to see and understand God. But the almighty is elusive, unpredictable, breaking away from our stultifying expectations. The Lord's invitation is that we always be alert. Be on the lookout. Keep your eyes and ears — and heart — open. God appears where you least expect.

Amen.

The Good Shepherd

Jesus offered the most famous metaphor for himself by elevating the most famous psalm. "I am the good shepherd." Perhaps he is also celebrating qualities we want to celebrate in a few weeks with our holiday of Mother's Day. Today's gospel and Psalm 23 are about shepherds, but they also describe qualities that make a great mother. In verse 11 Jesus says "I am the good shepherd. The good shepherd lays down his (or her) life for the sheep." How do shepherds and mothers compare?

Think about what a shepherd does. The shepherd does not make things or repair things, does not clock in at work, have a desk, go to meetings, or fill out reports. The shepherd does not do the things we usually associate with work.

A shepherd mostly watches. He leads, trusting that the sheep will follow. A shepherd escorts the sheep to places where the sheep will grow. A shepherd speaks to the sheep — wise shepherds know that speaking calmly and directly is much more effective than shouting. A shepherd makes sure nutritious food and safe water are available and often prepares the food if the sheep can't get to it themselves. A shepherd makes sure there is a place to sleep and that the flock stays together because they play better as a group and are safer together. A shepherd measures his or her life by the wellbeing of the flock. This sounds like a mother's life, too.

How about this quote describing some of God's creatures: "You're constantly on duty with them. When young they put anything in their mouths but in time become creatures of habit, uncreative in their food choice. They are given to listless wandering. They can be timid and stubborn. They can be frightened by little things although at other times nothing can move them. They have strong herd instincts which can make them dumb at times, following the leader blindly." Now — is that a description of a sheep or a teenager?

When Jesus called himself the good shepherd, he was praising the role of anyone, such as a mother, who watches over others and who shepherds other people. Jesus was not the only good shepherd — everyone is called to play this role for those around them who are weak or are learning or are in need.

Shepherds and mothers watch for our wellbeing, and they lead. They also know us best. Who better knows a child than his or her mother? And who knows the mother better than the infant? Studies at Yale Infancy Center show that babies in the third trimester of pregnancy recognize their mother's voice and soon after birth they recognize mothers' aromas and faces, showing this recognition by sucking hardest on pacifiers when mother is there.

Sheep also know their shepherds. During World War I the land that is today Israel was part of the Ottoman Empire controlled by Turkey. During the war one way the Turks controlled the local people was by combining many flocks of sheep into what you might call large herds controlled by Turkish shepherds. At war's end when the British took over that land the British promised to return to each of the original owners of sheep the same number of sheep that were taken from them. The shepherds protested, saying they wanted the very same sheep. "That's impossible," said the British. "There are thousands of sheep." "Watch us," said the shepherds. And then, one after another, the shepherds walked through the hills calling their sheep by name, and the sheep recognized their shepherd's voice and came running. This is why Jesus said, "[Their shepherd] goes before them, and the sheep follow him, for they know his voice." This gives extra credence to Jesus' words later in this chapter: "My sheep hear my voice, and I know them, and they follow me."

Mothers, shepherds, and Jesus alike must be both strong and gentle. Psalm 23 says, "Thy rod and thy staff, they comfort me." A shepherd's rod is a short club used to beat off attacking snakes or animals; it represents strength and authority. It's the primitive version of a gun. We even nickname handguns as "rods." Shepherds defend their sheep as fiercely as mothers defend babies.

A shepherd's staff is long; it's carefully smoothed and carved with a hook on the end. The hook is often used to gently draw a separated newborn ewe toward its mother. The shepherd dares not lift the ewe by hand for the odor of his hands might cause the mother to reject the newborn. How like a mother embracing a child or the Holy Spirit (the comforter) drawing people together in loving fellowship. The staff also taps the side of a sheep to turn it on a new path or simply to remind it that friend shepherd always is near if needed. Sounds like a good mother. Sounds like God.

Good mothers are good shepherds, with Christlike qualities. They watch and lead those for whom they care, and they know them. They also provide for them. Psalm 23 says, "He makes me lie down in green pastures; he leads me beside still waters." A sheep will only lie down when it is free of all fear. It is most content when it sees the shepherd nearby. Newborn babies usually sleep in the same room with Mom and Dad, and when they have their own rooms, they sleep best in their own beds. They need security. Lying on grass that is green assures the sleeping sheep there will be food in the morning when it awakes. Likewise, parents of neglected children whom they have adopted are encouraged to put nonperishable food in the child's room or backpacks so they won't fear hunger again. It's the green pasture of assurance. Christ our good shepherd says to his children, "I will give them eternal life, and they shall never perish, and no one shall snatch them from my hand." He reminds us the last will be first. Dozens of times in the Bible are words from the Christ and his followers about trust — "Fear not for I am with you; be not dismayed ... I shall never leave you nor forsake you ... I have learned in whatever state I am I will be content." Confidence in God's presence is our green pasture.

The mother, the shepherd, and Christ offer green pastures. And then "he leads me beside the still waters." Few things are more attractive than a fast-flowing mountain spring. It can be as intoxicating as a fast-moving life always seeking more glory and excitement. But sheep won't drink from fast-moving water. They either lick early morning dew or find a still water spring or they wait for the shepherd to draw water from a well and pour it into a low trough. Children also need "still waters" — family dinner routines, time to study quietly, and the comfort of knowing mom and dad are nearby. Adults are thirsty, too, and too often try to assuage their thirst by gulping in glory, knowledge, drugs, entertainment, travel, or unsavory friends. We are usually left panting and still thirsty. And then comes Christ. He says "Let anyone who is thirsty come to me and drink. Whoever believes in me, as scripture has said, 'Out of his mouth rivers of living waters will flow.'" For those willing to take the time and discipline to pray, study, worship, gaze at the world's beauty, meditate — in them the Holy Spirit will quietly grow. Of these still waters Saint Augustine said it so well — "Our souls are restless, O Lord, until they find their rest in thee."

Mothers, shepherds, and Christ also give encouragement. The word literally means "filled with courage." Several times in this gospel Jesus said, "I am the door" for the sheep. Sheep pens were usually made of stone and often did not have doors or gates. Instead, the shepherd lay at the entrance to the pen, sleeping there through the night. Sheep could not leave, and predators could not enter without confronting the shepherd. So, Jesus could add, "the good shepherd lays down his life for the sheep." He was both literally laying down at the gate and he was willing to sacrifice his life for the sheep he loved. The encouragement that sight gave the sheep helped explain the phrase in the psalm, "He restoreth my soul." At times all of us will feel discouraged or beaten down. Psalm 42 asks, "Why art thou cast down, O my soul? Why art thou disquieted within me? Hope thou in God..." The phrase "cast down" was not merely symbolic for a shepherd. In the language of shepherds, a sheep that lies down to sleep is cast down when it has rolled over on its back, legs in the air, and cannot stand again by itself. Often this is the healthiest looking sheep, large with a full growth of wool. Such a sheep may be too heavy for the shepherd to lift. He may have to shear the sheep to lighten it so he can lift it to its feet. That's like God stripping from us the possessions, pride, prejudice, or whatever weighs us down when we have fallen. Having the shepherd as the door lying nearby when you sleep gives encouragement that you will rise again when you fall. What mother would not do the same?

When Jesus said, "The good shepherd lays down his life for the sheep," he was foreshadowing the crucifixion. He was also describing the loyalty — what he called ownership — between shepherd and sheep. "He who is a hireling and not a shepherd, whose own the sheep are not, sees the wolf coming and leaves the sheep and flees... ." Often the good shepherd lays down a lifetime of savings to buy a small flock of sheep. All that he has is invested in them. Their wellbeing is his wellbeing. Their lives are entwined. This also foreshadows the church being called the "body of Christ." We not only represent Christ; we are Christ's possession. The height of sin is for people to vehemently reject and refuse the claim of God on our lives. To say "we belong" doesn't only mean there is a welcome place for us in heaven; it means we belong *to* the one who went to prepare a place for us there. "The Lord is my shepherd" means I belong to Lord. The Father and the faithful cannot be separated.

A few verses later in this tenth chapter of John, Jesus said, "I have other sheep, that are not of this fold; I must bring them also and they will heed my voice." Our emphasis and enjoyment of our closeness to God can promote the sin of exclusiveness. Jesus reminds us he will be the shepherd for all people. God had given Israel as "a light to the nations" (Isaiah 42). God is not our property any more than the shepherd is owned by the sheep.

Jesus' choice of words here was crucial. He said, "I have other sheep that are not of this fold... ." A sheep fold is the sheep kept together in one place, a sheep pen. When out of the pen they join other sheep folds to become a flock. They are not separated by the tangible or the geographic. In the same way, the bonds between Christians are greater than any division by race, nationality, distance, or culture. On this Mother's Day, remember there are more people in your family than those who live in your household. Throughout the world we are one people under God.

Jesus ends with the promise "I have come that you may have life and have it abundantly." This reflects the words of Psalm 23, "Surely goodness and mercy shall follow me all of the days of my life and I will dwell in the house of the Lord forever." Poorly managed sheep can destroy a pasture by overgrazing. But a good and smart shepherd leads the sheep to new pastures where they prosper. In fact, by eating otherwise noxious weeds and leaving behind nutritious excrement the sheep turn derelict fields into parks. And their practice of nibbling only the top of the grass keeps the field looking like a well-manicured lawn. In fact, some companies rent out sheep for lawn maintenance. They are called "lamb mowers." The company sets up a temporary fence around a property and for $250 a day rents a flock of sheep. It's a wonderfully tranquil sight. It's called a "sheep over." The phrase, "shall follow me all the days of your life" is literally true. For many days and months, a field is healthier if sheep and a good shepherd have been there.

The good shepherd — either Lord or mother — watches, understands, provides for, encourages, and points the way for abundant life. What a joy to be in that flock, that family.

Amen.

Imitation Of Christ

(The Peanuts cartoon referred to below can be found on the internet; it is from April 26, 1960.)

A great twentieth-century theologian who shaped the faith of many was Charles Schulz. You know him better as the creator of the *Peanuts* cartoons. In books such as *The Gospel According To Peanuts* and *The Parables Of Peanuts* Schulz was revealed as a proclaimer of Christian joy. Schulz grew up Lutheran in Saint Paul, Minnesota, and although he seldom attended church as an adult (he said worship was too much like a performance) he did always have a Bible and a picture of Jesus beside his drawing table. Schulz once said, "I contend that a cartoonist must be given a chance to do his own preaching." In the bulletin is an example of a sermon cartoon *(see above)*.

The message of this cartoon — Choose the life you want to emulate, and let it be high-minded, highly ambitious, with the height of love and service. If you are younger than fifty you may not remember Schweitzer. Seventy years ago, Albert Schweitzer was a Nobel-winning, world-famous theologian and musician (a rock-star organist!) who thought he could better serve humanity by going to medical school, becoming an MD and going to sub-Sahara Africa to open a free medical clinic. If his name doesn't ring a bell think of other famous celebrities who have been inspired to find their real value in life to be through charitable works outside their vocation — Taylor Swift, perhaps, Oprah Winfrey, or Paul Newman.

I mention these people and Charles' Schulz cartoon about imitating others because this is Mothers' Day. Children are great imitators. It is a mother's privilege to give them something great to imitate.

I also bring it up because imitation is the heart of today's gospel. During the Last Supper, Jesus was trying to explain his relationship to God the Father. He said, "If you know me, you will know my Father also. From now on you do know him and have seen him." He was saying he was the spitting image of God the Father, but Philip didn't get it. "Philip said to him, 'Lord, show us the Father and we will be satisfied.' Jesus said to him, 'Have I been with you all this time, Philip, and you still do not know me? Whoever has seen me has seen the Father.'"

Jesus was saying not only that he was a living, breathing audio-visual of the word of God but that he was God himself, so completely was he like the Father. He *was* and *is* one with the Father. Then he added, "the one who believes in me will also do the works that I do and, in fact, will do greater works than these... ." So, now *we* are to imitate Jesus. Like Father, like Son — like Son, like disciple.

We don't read the gospels to find laws for living. The Hebrews tried that earlier in the Bible and found that Leviticus and Deuteronomy were not best sellers. People don't crave laws. We hunger to live like the people we admire. Jesus did not teach with a lot of do's and don'ts. He taught by telling stories — parables — that invite us to find ourselves in the parable and live like the hero of the parable. And Jesus taught by his own example of wisdom, self-sacrifice, and love. He was the ultimate role model to the disciples, much as you mothers are to your children.

Jesus — and mothers — have competition as role models. Hollywood, Washington, the sports arena or golf course give us many people with carefully crafted images. They think our imitation will come at the ballot box, box office, or tee box. Sometimes it's hard to live up to the image. In the 1920s, Archibald Leach, a young English actor with a cockney accent came to America. He had been a street urchin on the rough streets of Bristol. In this country, he changed his accent and adopted a style of behaving cool and confident. He also adopted the stage name of Cary Grant. He could not escape the new name or the new style. He once said, "Everyone wants to be Cary Grant. Even I want to be Cary Grant." He spent his life imitating his image.

The New Testament continually tells us to imitate Jesus as he imitated the Father. "As I have loved you, so you must love one another," he said. At the Last Supper he said, "Now that I, your Lord and teacher, have washed your feet, you should wash one another's feet. I have set you an example that you should do as I have done for you." Saint Paul, in Ephesians 5:12 told us, "Be imitators of God, therefore, as dearly beloved children." In 1 Corinthians 3:18, Paul told us such imitation makes us who we are. "And we, who with unveiled faces all reflect the Lord's glory, we are being transformed into his likeness." Study Christ closely, Paul said (that's what he means by unveiled faces) and we will become like Christ. And it's not only Christ we imitate. It's Christ's star disciples. Paul says in Philippians 3:17: "Brethren, join in imitating me, and mark those who so live as you have an example in us." In 1 Corinthians 11:1 Paul says, "Follow my example, as I follow the example of Christ." The word "follow" and the word "imitate" are the same word in Greek, *typos*, which gives the word type. There is a Christian type, Paul is saying — forgiven and forgiving, loved and loving. On top of that, Paul said we must be people that others imitate. He wrote to his protégé in 1 Timothy 4:12b: "… set an example for the believers in speech, in life, in love, in faith, and in purity." The imitation trail is like a line of falling dominoes from the Father through the Son and through the disciples right down to us.

The disciples were very content knowing they didn't always have to try to be original. "We love because he first loved us," said 1 John 4:19. In 1 Peter 2:23 this apostle spoke of Jesus, "When they hurled insults at him, he did not retaliate; when he suffered, he made no threats." In 1 Corinthians 4:12-13 the apostle Paul came right back, "When *we* are cursed, we bless; when *we* are persecuted, we answer kindly." Like Father, like Son; like Son, like disciples.

Imitation is not only the highest form of flattery; it is the essence of faith. Ever worn a WWJD bracelet? WWJD stands for "What Would Jesus Do?" The most important spiritual book of the Middle Ages was titled, *The Imitation of Christ*. (Heaven's sake — even this sermon's title is an imitation.) The book of Acts tells us that the followers of Jesus in Antioch were so intent on being like the Lord that the people of Antioch gave them what they thought was a witty nickname. Acts 11:26: "And in Antioch the disciples were for the first time called Christians." The word means imitator, a copycat Christ.

Who in your life do you want to imitate? Is there someone who is your role model? Hopefully, Jesus is your greatest role model. That's why I'm so eager to promote prayer and Bible study so that the vision of Jesus' actions are front and center in our minds as a model. He was patient with sinners but impatient with the self-righteous. He loved to celebrate people at wedding parties and would not let his host be embarrassed by running out of wine. He embraced children that the world ignored. His friends were the last people you'd expect in church — rough fishermen (Peter and Andrew), a shady politician (Matthew the tax collector), a bounty hunter (Paul), a woman of the streets (Mary Magdalene), and a socialite (Joanna, wife of Herod's chief of staff). Jesus said, "Bring them on. As long as they're not full of themselves I'll fill them with my Spirit and transform them." He did transform them so that in time they tried to be like Jesus.

My graduate school advisor, theologian Harvey Cox, once spoke to a gathering of 600 Christian leaders. He told them the gospel story of Jesus being called to resuscitate the daughter of a wealthy Roman. As Jesus was going to the Roman's house, a woman with an illness reached out from the crowd and touched his robe. He felt her touch, turned around, and asked, 'Who touched me?' The woman came forward and begged him to cure her, and he did. Then he went on to the house of the Roman whose daughter has died.

After telling this story, Cox asked the audience with whom in the story did they identify. When he asked who identified with the ill woman, about a hundred hands went up. When he asked who identified with the anxious Roman father, more raised their hands. When he asked who identified with the curious crowd, most raised their hands. But when he asked who identified with Jesus, only six people raised their hands.

Something was wrong there. Of 600 more or less professional Christians, only one out of a hundred identified with Jesus. Maybe more actually did but were afraid to raise their hands lest they seemed arrogant. But again, something is wrong with our concept of Christianity if it seems arrogant to identify with Jesus. That is exactly what we are supposed to do! We're supposed to identify with Jesus, act like Jesus, and be like Jesus. It's the heart of faith.

But we should also look to people who have been shaped by Christ, the Albert Schweitzer people, and ask what would they do if they were in our place right now.

I remember some years ago when there was tension and deviousness among people in my church and I was trying to be as high-minded and loving as I could be. My young son, who loved movies, sensed my stress. Andrew said, "You can handle it, Dad. I always think of you as Atticus Finch." I gasped. I had never told Andrew that this Gregory Peck character in *To Kill A Mockingbird* had been my secret role model for fifty years. And I'm not alone. The American Film Institute named Atticus Finch the greatest movie hero of all time. That institute knew we need heroes.

And it's more than the Atticus Finch character. I wanted to be Gregory Peck! Peck had a flourishing career going in the mid 1940s — nominated for best actor in only his second movie — when he risked everything because of his ideals. He was offered the lead in a movie about anti-Semitism. His friends said he should stay away from a movie about discrimination against Jews — it would destroy his career. But Peck believed in the movie's message and the movie, *Gentleman's Agreement*, was a hit. After that Peck decided to use his career to advance his causes. He made *Man In The Grey Flannel Suit* about materialism and greed; he made *12 O'Clock High* about the real cost of war, and *To Kill A Mockingbird* about racism. And in the midst of it all, he took a year off from acting to chair the American Cancer Society and did another stint as president of the Academy of Motion Pictures Arts. When Peck was asked who *his* role model in life was, he said, "The Good Samaritan."

Who do you imitate? Whose image is unconsciously imbedded in your mind, guiding your actions and mouthing your words before you speak them? Choose wisely. And remember this children's poem:

> *There are little eyes upon you*
> *They are watching night and day*
> *There are little ears that quickly*
> *Take in every word you say.*
> *There are little hands all eager*
> *To do anything you do;*
> *And a little child is dreaming*
> *Of the day he'll be like you!*

Amen.

Sixth Sunday of Easter

Acts 17:22-31, 1 Peter 3:13-22, John 14:15-21

Whispering The Lyrics

In musical days, before Elvis was king and when beetles were just bugs — that is, in the early 1950s — there was a great blues master named Jimmy Reed. A son of a sharecropper, Reed brought into the popular rock-and-roll mainstream the wild rhythm-and-blues he learned in the Mississippi Delta. Reed was a major influence on Bob Dylan, Elvis Presley, and the Rolling Stones. Many budding rock bands tried to imitate the eccentric Reed's songs "Bright Lights, Big City," "Big Boss Man," and "Cousin Peaches." Few could capture the hypnotic wails of his harmonica, the throbbing of his guitar, the moans of his words.

Today if you listen closely to an old 45 rpm record by Reed you might notice something strange. Listen carefully and you might catch, faintly in the background, the soft voice of a woman murmuring in advance the next verse of the song. It seems Reed was so absorbed in the bluesy beat and hypnotic guitar riffs of his music that he would forget the words of the songs he had written. To feed him the lyrics was his wife, Mary, whom he called Mama. She would sit in the background during recording sessions whispering coming stanzas into his ear as he sang.

Whispering our lyrics — on Mother's Day, isn't that what good mothers do? Our mothers' wisdom may not seem profound; mostly good sense reminders of what we already know. "Do your best in whatever you start … Aim high with ambition… Others first… Be understanding and forgiving… The door to home is always open… Don't worry — you're always loved." In a world screaming for our attention, our allegiance, our action, these are words to remind us who and whose we are. Like Jimmy Reed, we need a loving lady whispering life's lyrics in our ears.

That image also helps us understand today's gospel. In his final sermon to the disciples, hours before he was killed, Jesus told them the Holy Spirit was coming. The role of the Holy Spirit was to whisper the lyrics of the gospel in their ears. The word for the Spirit that Jesus used here was *paraclete.* We often translate that as helper or comforter. A closer meaning is encourager, that is, one who gives us courage. The Latin translation is *fortis,* which gives us the words fort and fortify and means wisely brave. For the three years that he was with the disciples, Jesus was the one to instill in them the courage, coach them with the right words, steady them with unfailing love, and teach them the joyful truth. But with him leaving, that role was handed over to the Holy Spirit. "If you love me, you will keep my commandments, and I will ask the Father and he will give you another advocate to be with you forever. This is the Spirit of truth."

The purpose of the Holy Spirit is like the role of the good mother — to remind us as children of the truth, jogging the memories of Christ's followers to remember who we are and whose we are. The Spirit whispers in our ears the lyrics of the never-ending hymn of faithful, loving obedience.

There is a wonderful nuance in Jesus' words in verses 5 and 6, "Father... I have made your name known... ." As you may know, for Jews God's personal name, "Yahweh" was so sacred that no one spoke the name for fear it would be profaned. Look throughout the Old Testament and you will see all four letters of the word "LORD" are capitalized. That is because that word LORD was substituted for the personal name of God which no one was worthy to speak or spell. In ancient times for God's personal name only the consonants JHWH were written in the Bible. The person reading would instead say the word "Lord." Jesus was telling the disciples he was so close to God that Jesus could call God, "Father." And he prayed that the disciples could be that intimate with God, also. "Holy Father, keep them in your name, which you gave to me, that they may be one, as we are one." What keeps them together as one? It is the Holy Spirit's whisper, calling, and encouraging.

I know, the Spirit is usually advertised in flashier terms: the Spirit prompted speaking in strange tongues; the Spirit lifted our spirits in euphoria; the Spirit miraculously healed. And those may be done on the side. But mostly, the Spirit whispered the loving gospel lyrics into the ears of the forgetful faithful.

Remember the Old Testament story of the time Elijah obeyed God by confronting the evil Queen Jezebel with her sins? The enraged Jezebel put a price on the old prophet's head and he, disillusioned, headed into the desert to sulk and shake his fist at God for setting him up. God's angel told Elijah to stand outside his cave to hear the voice of the almighty. And the Lord passed as a huge storm that tears apart nearby mountains. But God did not speak in the wind. Then came an earthquake, but God did not speak in the earthquake. Then a fire, but still no God. Finally came a still, small voice. And you knew it —in that whisper was God. God comforted the old prophet and encouraged him to go back and do the ministry he knew he should be doing.

We need that still, small voice — we need that Holy Spirit (we need mothers) because we are easily discouraged and frightfully forgetful. And we need that steady voice because the world is so full of danger and anger. In today's first reading we see life when the Spirit has come. It's the church in the book of Acts.

A story might best explain the early church. Many years ago at the University of Wisconsin there was a club for promising writers. All club members were male, and all had shown literary talent. At each meeting one member would read an essay he had written, and the others would dissect it. Their critiques were scorching. Line by line students pointed out problems with no mercy. So nasty were the sessions that the members called themselves "The Stranglers." The women literary students on campus thought there was a better way to develop writing skills. They formed a club they called "The

Wranglers" after those cowboys who rounded up stray cattle and guided them back to the herd. Like their male counterparts these women would read their writings at meetings and offer feedback. But their reflections were thoughtful, gentle, positive, and kind, like whispers of the Holy Spirit. They lifted each other up and encouraged all.

Twenty years later, a university researcher looked at the careers of the members of both groups. Not one of the bright young men of "The Stranglers" had achieved a literary reputation. But "The Wranglers" had a number of prominent writers, some nationally known. What was the difference? The carping Stranglers cut each other down. The whispers of "The Wranglers" lifted each other up. One choked life and the other enhanced it.

Then there was the church. Stranglers or Wranglers?

You and I live in an age of anger. People think the best way to respond to problems is to criticize and complain, as if that would improve things. How different it was in the early church after the Holy Spirit came. The whisper and wind of the Spirit blew through those Christians. Their goal was to invite, not to incite. They had a sense of excitement, love, and purpose. They shared possessions, ate together, and worshiped together. They were creators, not critics.

And what happened when the world tried to strangle them? An amazing thing! Those first Christians actually treated their attackers with graciousness, the same graciousness they showed each other. Saint Peter, leader of the early church, gave his people their guiding principle. In today's second reading he wrote, "In your hearts sanctify Christ as Lord. Always be ready to make a defense to anyone who demands from you an accounting of the hope that is in you; yet do it with gentleness and reverence." He put on paper the encouraging whispers of the Holy Spirit.

Peter's word that we translate as "make a defense" is from the Greek word, *apologia*. We translate the word as "explanation," "account," or "defense." Here is where we get the English word *apologetics*, which is a reasoned articulation of the faith and a defense against any attacks mounted against it. It is a word used in first-century Greece to refer to a legal case argued before judge and jury. But *apologia* is also where we get the word apology. Peter was saying your explanations should be designed to heal old wounds. How do we do that? At the heart of the word *apologia* is *logos*. *Logos* means words, what we say. But a logo is also an image. Think of the Nike® swish, the McDonald's® golden arches, the black or white apple of Apple® computers. People watch your image, your appearance. They see your patience, your smiles, your steady gaze, and they recognize in your gentleness and love the image of Christ.

Peter's attitude was contagious. Saint Paul was by nature a fiery, combative person — a strangler, not a wrangler. Remember his job as a bounty hunter was arresting Christians that they might be killed. Yet from Peter and Barnabas even Paul could see the church's gentleness and hear the Spirit's whispers. In today's first reading it says Paul went to Athens as a missionary and there saw pagan statues all around. The old Paul would have been fire and brimstone, knocking the idols over and condemning their makers to hell. But this kinder, gentler Paul says softly, 'Well, I see that you are religious around here. Let me tell you about my God.' And those tough Athenians listened and learned. Peter and Paul were saints, and a saint is someone who has heard the Spirit's whisper and passes it on to others.

How do you approach life? Are you a strangler or a wrangler? Is your demeanor meaner? Do you incite or invite? Are you a *reactor* who complains or an *actor*, a doer of the positive, who defends the hope within you with gentleness and reverence. Listen carefully. The Spirit is whispering in your ear.

Amen.

What Patients Need Most

A young woman was walking through a park with her trusty old Polaroid® camera swinging from her shoulder. Suddenly she heard footsteps behind her and then two men grabbed her camera and ran off. She screamed. A minute later a police officer arrived on foot. She pointed the direction the thieves had gone, and he pursued. Meanwhile, in a wooded grove a quarter mile away the thieves were checking the strange camera. Something was wrong. Each thief took a picture of the other but both pictures came out blank. Disgusted, they tossed the blank pictures aside and decided to head to a pawn shop. On the way they kept taking pictures of the park as they tried to understand this camera. Every picture was blank, so they threw each one away. At the edge of the park the officer came upon them taking a photo of a squirrel. In the policeman's hands were the two now-developed pictures of the thieves as well as all of their discarded park photos that he had followed like a trail of crumbs. The young thieves didn't realize that a Polaroid® camera takes several minutes to develop each shot. With a Polaroid® you have to wait.

For forty days after the Resurrection Jesus taught the disciples and promised the Holy Spirit would come to them. Then, at the Ascension his last words to them were "You must wait… until the power from above comes down upon you."

Jesus said to them, *"Wait."* Imagine how the disciples must have chaffed at Jesus' orders. These were men of action and they had witnessed the resurrection and the ascension, the most awesome events in history. Why wait for this invisible Spirit? Why not jump into action right away?

We can empathize with them, can't we? None of us likes to wait. We live in an instant gratification world with our minute rice and microwave ovens. All Christmas shopping can be done online in an hour. Want a suntan? Forget the beach and the sun — twelve minutes in a tanning booth once a week will do it. Today you can fly from New York to Chicago in under two hours; a century ago it took 24 hours by train and two centuries ago it took three weeks on horseback. We are an impatient people.

Yet Jesus seemed to think there was a reason for the disciples to wait for the Holy Spirit. They needed a spiritual maturation. Sometimes we wonder why God doesn't work more quickly in our lives. We wonder why our prayers are not answered according to our timetable. One of the Bible's great lessons is that God's schedule is not our schedule. We have to wait. Circumstances may not be right yet. We may not be right yet. Paul wrote "We know that for those who love God all things work together for good, for those who are called according to his purpose." He never said it would be fast.

"Wait on the Lord", wrote the psalmist, "be of good courage, and he shall strengthen thy heart..." "Those who wait upon the Lord... shall inherit the earth."

From the pen of Isaiah: "They that wait upon the Lord shall renew thy strength." The word "wait" appears more than 100 times in scripture. Sometimes there is nothing we can do. But Paul promised, "...our Lord Jesus Christ shall sustain you to the end...[for] God is faithful."

Mee Spousler, a Pennsylvania homemaker, put her three-year-old son down for a nap. He wouldn't sleep so she put him in her bed and lay down beside him to encourage him to rest. She fell asleep; he did not. When she woke, he was in the chair at the end of the bed looking at her.

"Luke, what are you doing?"

"I'm playing God," he replied.

"Playing God?" she asked.

"Yes," he explained. "I'm watching over you while you sleep."

It takes humility to wait. When we have to wait, we admit there are some things not under our control — recuperation from surgery, for instance, or the grief process, or a young person learning responsibility. Shakespeare put it like this: "How poor are they that have no patience. What wound did ever heal but by degrees?" In the hospital the *patient* patient heals best.

Patience is not always pleasant. Patience is from the Latin word *pati* which means to suffer. After the time of Kings David and Solomon, Israel was sinful for hundreds of years and God allowed the Babylonians to conquer them. Israel spent a generation in captivity in Babylon. Sitting as serfs along the Tigris and Euphrates Rivers some wondered if God had forgotten them. But God had not forgotten and with deliverance came a new name — Judaism. Patience is not always pleasant. Jesus had an emotional high in his baptism with God the Father saying, "This is my Son; with him I am well pleased." But then the Lord struggled alone in the wilderness temptation for forty days wondering if he could live up to the Father's expectations. That forty-day trial steeled him for the next three years of ministry ending on Calvary. Patience is not always pleasant.

Patience is endurance. Sometimes it is a testing which can mean suffering. James wrote: "Count it all joy, my brothers, when you meet trials of various kinds, for you know that the testing of your faith produces steadfastness. And let steadfastness have its full effect, that you may be perfect and complete, lacking in nothing."

Other times it may feel like loneliness or boredom, even the sense of being abandoned. The poet John Milton in the 1650s went blind. He was only 45-years old and felt useless. He spent his days in prayer and thought and composing poems he would dictate for others to pen. The end result would be his classic work *Paradise Lost*. On the way, his Sonnet 19 ended with the epic words "They also serve who only stand and wait."

Time waiting is not time wasted. Wise people can wait. Wise people are wary of instant gratification. Benjamin Disraeli said, "Patience is a necessary ingredient of genius." Warren Buffet was a great advocate for patience. He was thinking of financial investments, of course, of the power of compound interest to grow wealth, but his wisdom was good for all instant-gratification people. Buffett once said, "No matter how great the talent or effort, some things just take time. You can't produce a baby in one month by getting nine women pregnant."

To learn patience takes discipline. The great author Victor Hugo was impatient by nature. He especially loved attending parties with his friends, which prevented him from writing. He decided to lock up his formal clothes so he would have nothing to wear on evenings out and consequently be unable to party. All he kept was a gray shawl that he wore every day until he completed his masterpiece, *The Hunchback of Notre Dame*. Locking away his evening clothes was the discipline that helped him create the masterpiece.

Patience takes discipline.

The marshmallow test is a classic psychology experiment first conducted by researchers at Stanford University in the late 1960s. Researchers were trying to identify the processes that underlie self-control in preschoolers when they face temptation.

In the marshmallow experiment, preschoolers had a choice between eating one marshmallow immediately or waiting for a greater reward of two marshmallows later. The children were then measured on how long they could wait to eat the first marshmallow. The researchers found that the preschoolers who could wait longest were happier and more successful in adolescence, with higher SAT scores, better social cognition, and more emotional coping skills. They also had greater self-control, were less prone to temptation, and were less distracted when concentrating. They had learned the patience of delayed gratification.

Our ancestors in faith understood. God told Abraham and Sarah they would have descendants as numerous as the stars. Did they become discouraged in the quarter century between that promise and the birth of their only son, Isaac? We know Moses was frustrated that it took God forty years to refine the Exodus Israelites in the wilderness before they completed the mere 200-mile journey from Egypt to Israel. God was not pleased with Moses' impatience and only allowed him to see the Promised Land from a distance and not to enter it. And what about Paul after his conversion who spent at least a dozen years in reflection and study before beginning missionary work.

God has all eternity at divine disposal. God will not be rushed. The great colonial pastor Cotton Mather prayed for religious revival several hours every day for twenty years; the Great Awakening began the year he died. The British Empire abolished slavery as abolitionist leader William Wilberforce lay on his deathbed, exhausted from his nearly 55-year campaign against human bondage. J.K. Rowling received dozens of rejection letters before the first *Harry Potter* book was published, and she still keeps her first rejection letter on her refrigerator. Prince Charles of the United Kingdom was 73 years old when he was crowned King Charles III — the longest serving heir apparent in history for that realm and the longest job interview. When German missionaries first went to Tanzania 130 years ago, they converted only a few hundred people in the first decades; today two-thirds of Tanzanians are Christian. As C.S. Lewis has written: "The principal part of faith is patience."

Jeremiah once wrote: "For I know the plans I have for you," declares the LORD, "plans to prosper you and not to harm you, plans to give you hope and a future." Interesting — the prophet did not say that *we* know the plans God has for us. Ours is a God of revelation and revelation can take time. Faith is not memorizing the particulars of our religion. Faith is trusting the blank photo of the future will develop in time and God will be in it. As the writer of Hebrews said: "Faith is the assurance of things hoped for and the conviction of things not seen."

Amen.

"I Know Nothing — Except...."

(Images of the people mentioned in the two World War II stories can be found online and shown on the sanctuary screen. For a video of this sermon's end see https://youtu.be/kjBsQf_jlIQ.)

Congratulations. You've come to worship on the Sunday with the most confusing gospel reading of the whole year. This is called Jesus' "High Holy Prayer." Jesus and the disciples were at the Last Supper. This prayer was directed by Jesus to his Father in heaven, but the disciples were listening, and Jesus was telling them what he expected from them after he had ascended to heaven. It was a tall order.

Part of the challenge in reading this today was that different Bible translations used different words. This is the longest prayer in the Bible and Jesus prayed that God the Father would help the disciples after he was gone. But what did "help" really mean? In the last verse we read today — John 17:11 — the Revised Standard Version of the Bible reported Jesus asked the Father, "keep them in thy name." The Jerusalem Bible (a popular Catholic translation from sixty years ago) had Jesus say, "keep them true to your name." But then, Today's English Version translation makes the same words read, "keep them safe." Both the New English Version and the New International Version say that Jesus asked the Father to "protect them." Phillips Translation is "protect [them] by the power of thy name." The Living Bible simply says, "keep them in your own care."

So, what was Jesus asking of the Father — that the disciples stay loyal to God (that is, stay "in thy name") or that the disciples be safe and protected? Can you do both? The disciples certainly were not safe after Jesus ascended to heaven. Tradition says that eleven of the twelve disciples died violently. Judas hung himself, ten others were martyred by the authorities. Only John lived to a ripe old age, writing the book of Revelation, but John was writing while under Roman guard in lonely exile. Except for Judas, all the disciples stayed in God's name as missionaries but none of them stayed safe.

Jesus' last words to the disciples at the Ascension explored this tension between staying in God's name and staying safe. Jesus told them, "When the Holy Spirit comes upon you, you will be filled with power, and you will be witnesses for me in Jerusalem, in all of Judea and Samaria, and to the ends of the earth." They could be confident doing ministry in a dangerous world because God was about to give them a power far beyond anything they had ever experienced.

How do you explain this power the disciples will have? Eighty-five years ago, cartoonist Stan Lee created a comic book character that caught the imagination of the nation. Poor, orphaned Billy Bateson could turn himself into Captain Marvel just by uttering once magical word — SHAZAM! Shazam actually was an acronym stating all of the powers he gained as Captain Marvel. SHAZAM stood for Solomon's wisdom, Hercules' strength, Achilles' courage, Zeus' power, Atlas' stamina, and Mercury's speed.

The power of the Holy Spirit goes far beyond those gifts granted Captain Marvel. The Spirit is Christ alive in the disciples and alive in us — Immanuel forever. All the works the disciples had seen Jesus do preaching, teaching, inspiring, comforting, healing, increasing our resources (loaves and fishes) these disciples would be able to do. And they will be doing them in the midst of life's struggles and hurts.

Then Jesus asked for one other gift. In verse 13 he prayed that the disciples "may have the full measure of my joy within them." The power of the Spirit was to keep them loyal to the audacious mission of living "in my name," that is, as Christians, a title that literally means an imitator of Christ, and that

Spirit was to keep them safe in a dangerous world. And, if that was not enough, they were to exude joy. Walk life's circus tight-rope, always moving ahead on the tightrope precisely as Christ wanted, always in danger of falling, and always bringing joy to the people below who are watching. Be an unwed, pregnant, refugee teenage girl, owing taxes, stuck in a stable with smelly animals, and there give birth to your first child...the world might not think that was safe or sane, but the angels singing above that Bethlehem stable offered the sights and sounds of eternal joy. Being executed on a cross between two thieves is the worst fate imaginable. But if you were obedient to the voice you heard the night before in the Garden of Gethsemane, you would leave behind you an empty tomb three days later. There is more to safety than avoiding danger. There is a rising above.

Several times in this Last Supper prayer, Jesus told the disciples to be his witness, telling others of him. The biblical Greek word for witness is *marturia* — martyr. So routinely did Christ's followers die as punishment for being witnesses, preaching the gospel, that we have given a new definition to the word martyr. In the fifth chapter of the book of Acts it reports that Peter and the other apostles were taken before Jerusalem's high council, the Sanhedrin, and there publicly whipped and ordered not to speak of Christ again. They ignored those orders, of course. Verse 41 says, "As the apostles left the council, they were happy, because God had considered them *worthy* to suffer disgrace for the sake of Jesus."

When you witness for God's glory you may suffer. And when you suffer proclaiming confidence that God's power is behind you, then you are worthy witnesses. And when you are worthy witness there will be a radiance, a joy, surrounding you.

A true story: In 1939, the Nazi army invaded Poland. They began a campaign of terror against Polish Jews, killing thousands and forcing hundreds of thousands more into ghettos. A local businessman Oskar Schindler, offered to hire a number of Jewish workers to work at very low wages in his factories. Among other things they were to make ammunition for the

German army. In time, he hired 1,300 Jews. Through bribery and black-market connections, this crooked womanizer was able to keep his employees from death in concentration camps. In time, God worked on Schindler's heart and he saw the horrors of Nazism. While he was convincing his Nazi bosses that his factory was indispensable for the war effort, he was allowing his workers to make faulty cannon shells that would not fire properly.

On Schindler's famous list of Jewish workers was Number 173, a man named Leopold "Poldek" Pfefferberg. After the war, this Poldek, as he was called, moved to Los Angeles, and opened a luggage store. But he felt his purpose in life was to witness to the world what Schindler and his workers had done. He called Schindler "a modern Noah." Poldek spent decades searching for a writer who could tell their story. Finally, he convinced author Thomas Keneally to tackle the story. Keneally said with a smile that in 1980 Poldek "bullied me" into writing the book *Schindler's Ark*. Poldek told the author, "(Schindler) was Jesus Christ, and although he was Jesus Christ, a saint he wasn't." Once the book was published it won awards. Then Poldek began badgering Steven Spielberg to turn it into a movie. Spielberg bought the film rights but waited ten years before making the movie. He felt he was not mature enough for such a heavy subject.

When Spielberg did tackle making the movie, he chose to film on location in Poland. He hired descendants of Nazi guards to be extras in the film in the roles of their ancestors, and descendants of Schindler's Jewish workers to be the factory workers. Not surprisingly, on the film set there was tension between descendants of victims and victimizers. Then the German Christians playing the guards asked if they could respectfully watch the Jewish actors in a Hanukkah meal held in their hotel during the filming. These Jewish extras said, "No, don't watch us. We want you to *join* us in the Hannukah meal." And so it was, in the shadows of a concentration camp Christians and Jews celebrated God's power of love to keep people safe in God. When the movie premiered in 1993, it won seven Oscars (no pun intended) and was hailed as one of the greatest films ever made. Schindler, Poldek, Keneally, Spielberg and all of those actors — each witnessing in his own way to God's power to be in God's name, *as well as* to be safe in a cruel world, *and* to be joyous.

How do we with joy rise above our sick world? Our second reading today tells us. Peter writes, "Rejoice insofar as you are sharing Christ's sufferings, so that you may also be glad and shout for joy when his glory is revealed." Peter says the best way to rise above suffering is to rejoice — laugh at the suffering. Sometimes the Bible says suffering is merely to be endured. "Weeping may last for the night, but joy comes in the morning," says Psalm 30. More often, though, the Bible says suffering is to humanize us, to make us stronger, wiser, deeper. That's why Jesus in the beatitudes blesses the strangest people — losers mostly — the meek, the grieving, the poor, those hungering for righteous judgment. In their hunger they are the ones most open to find God. Thomas Aquinas said, "God permits suffering in order to draw forth a greater good."

You've heard the saying "No Pain, No Gain." In the same way, no suffering, no triumph. No sadness, no joy — no hunger, no drooling in anticipation of a Thanksgiving meal. A constancy of comfort and ease and success is a terrible thing. Passengers on cruise ships after nine beautiful sunsets and 89 invigorating games of shuffleboard begin to ask the crew hopefully, "Do you think we will have a storm?" In embracing the cross we gain the strength to keep in God's name and rise above the suffering. A life that is always comfortable dulls us, lulls us. Suffering forces us to think about what is important, to be centered on Christ. Saint Paul, who was often beaten and imprisoned could have been bitter. But Paul wrote, "I decided to know nothing among you except Christ and him crucified"(1 Corinthians 2:2) Paul focused. Remember Lincoln's line, "People are about as happy as they make up their minds to be." That's what Paul is saying. "I decided — it's my choice.

I know nothing except Christ and him crucified."It wasn't mind over matter. It was mind over misery. Happiness and joy were his focus, his way to overcome, to rise above, to be kept in Christ's name.

Byron Janis was a world-famous concert pianist who died early in 2024. The society page of the paper told us he was actor Gary Cooper's son-in-law. The art page told us he was a brilliant musician. However, for fifty years Byron Janis suffered from excruciating arthritis. Every movement of his hands was painful. But he also was involved in mind-over-matter studies. In a national radio interview he said, "As soon as I get involved with music — no more pain." Focus! "I decided to know nothing except..." Joy and beauty are decisions.

Here is the story of five men who made the decision sixty years ago to answer suffering with joy. John Banner was Jewish from Austria. When Hitler took over Austria in 1938, Banner was playing summer stock in a theater in Switzerland. While his parents perished in a concentration camp, 28-year-old John escaped to America. There he went to law school. He supported himself as a master of ceremony for various events, but his German accent was so heavy that he had to learn his lines in English phonetically. Always he was haunted by the memory of those camps where his relatives died.

Werner Klemperer was a German Jew, a concert violinist and conductor. His father, Otto, was a famous conductor. Just before he watched his relatives being rounded up for concentration camps Otto got permission to take his family and teenage Werner on a concert tour of America. Otto never returned. When Werner returned to Germany in 1945 it was as an officer in the US army looking for relatives who died in the death camps.

Robert Clary was French. As a teenager during the war, he served in the French Resistance and was captured and served the rest of the war in a German POW camp where his parents and thirteen brothers and sisters died. Like the others he immigrated to America and hungered to overcome the bitter memories of those camps. Clary once said, "I don't hold a grudge because that's a great waste of time. Yes, there's something dark in the human soul. That's why when you find good people, you cherish them."

Richard Dawson saw World War II from a different perspective. As an eight-year-old in England he watched as German planes rained bombs on his hometown of Gosport. He, too, had relatives who fought and died or spent the war in POW camps. How do you overcome such suffering?

Ivan Dixon is the only one of the five not from war-torn Europe. But Dixon knew his own share of suffering. A poor African-American from Harlem in the 1940s and 1950s, several of his relatives spent time in prison. As an adult Dixon wanted to fight back. He wanted to fight racism. He joined Martin Luther King Jr's civil rights movement. In the early '70s he even became national president of the civil rights organization of his profession, the Negro Actors for Action.

You see, all five of these men were actors. In 1965, they met for the first time when they were asked to be in a new television show. The show was set in the one place they all knew and dreaded — a prison. All hesitated but then they realized this was a chance to confront their painful memories and rise above them. For this show was to be different. It was set in a Prisoner of War camp, and it was a comedy. They could fight the horrors of their memories with the power of humor because in their studio contract they stipulated that the bad guys must never win and the good in people must be celebrated. And so was born the popular show Hogan's Heroes with Ivan Dixon, Richard Dawson, and Robert Clary as Allied POWs, and as the camp's guards were Werner Klemperer as bumbling Colonel Klink and John Banner as fumbling Sergeant Shultz. "I know nothing, *nothing* — except Christ and him crucified."

Now the question is for you. How have you kept in God's name, rising above suffering with joy?

Amen.

www.ingramcontent.com/pod-product-compliance
Lightning Source LLC
Chambersburg PA
CBHW022028090426
42739CB00006BA/337